Math Rock

Forthcoming in the series:

Vaporwave by Kirk Walker Graves
Feminist Anarcho-Punk by June Amelia Rose
Field Recordings by Marc Weidenbaum
Neue Deutsche Welle by Claudia Lonkin
Soul-Folk by Ashawnta Jackson
Shoegaze by Ryan Pinkard

Math Rock

Jeff Gomez

GENRE
A 33⅓ SERIES

BLOOMSBURY ACADEMIC
NEW YORK • LONDON • OXFORD • NEW DELHI • SYDNEY

BLOOMSBURY ACADEMIC
Bloomsbury Publishing Inc
1385 Broadway, New York, NY 10018, USA
50 Bedford Square, London, WC1B 3DP, UK
29 Earlsfort Terrace, Dublin 2, Ireland

BLOOMSBURY, BLOOMSBURY ACADEMIC and the Diana logo
are trademarks of Bloomsbury Publishing Plc

First published in the United States of America 2024

Bloomsbury Publishing Inc does not have any control over, or
responsibility for, any third-party websites referred to or in this book.
All internet addresses given in this book were correct at the time of going
to press. The author and publisher regret any inconvenience caused if
addresses have changed or sites have ceased to exist, but can accept no
responsibility for any such changes.

Whilst every effort has been made to locate copyright holders
the publishers would be grateful to hear from any person(s)
not here acknowledged.

A catalog record for this book is available from the Library of Congress.

ISBN: PB: 979-8-7651-0337-1
        ePDF: 979-8-7651-0339-5
        eBook: 979-8-7651-0338-8

Series: Genre: A 33 1/3 Series

Typeset by Integra Software Service Pvt. Ltd.
Printed and bound in Great Britain

To find out more about our authors and books visit www.bloomsbury.com
and sign up for our newsletters.

To Van and June, who came from Chicago

Contents

Prologue: Friday Night in Chicago viii

1   **All Is Number: What Is Math Rock?** 1

2   **Breadcrumb Trail: The Origins of Math Rock** 9

3   **Rollerblade Success Story: A Short History of Math Rock** 25

4   **Oh Messy Life: Genres Related to Math Rock** 41

5   **Savage Composition: Writing Math Rock** 57

6   **Tremolo + Delay: Playing Math Rock** 73

7   **Here Comes Everybody: The Internet and Math Rock** 89

8   **Cognitive Emancipation: Listening to Math Rock** 105

Epilogue: Friday Night in Sacramento 117
Ten Essential Tracks 124
References 128

Prologue: Friday Night in Chicago

It's 1999 and Don Caballero takes the stage at the Fireside Bowl, an old bowling alley located in Logan Square on the city's northwest side. The building had originally been an ice factory before being turned into a bowling alley in the forties. It's still a bowling alley. However, since it started hosting all ages punk shows in 1994, crowds come mostly for the music rather than to bowl. The room can hold eight hundred people, but for most concerts the audience hovers around three hundred. Tonight, despite the fact that Don Cab played the day before across town at the Empty Bottle, the place is packed.

The shallow stage stands just a few feet off the ground. There are no spotlights. The room's illuminated only by a few bright bulbs in the low ceiling. Hanging just a couple feet from the heads of the musicians, the ceiling is made of uneven, stained tiles. Behind the band is a wall of peeling paint. The young crowd's wearing mostly T-shirts, hoodies, or light jackets. It had been a cool day in Chicago, barely above sixty degrees. The hot and muggy summer finally seems to be over. But in a week the heat will be back, temperatures yet again rising above eighty.

The group, a trio, looks like any other indie rock band from the nineties. Drums, bass, guitar, thrift store clothes. The only thing different is the lack of microphones. In most groups, the guitarist is the singer. Occasionally it's the bassist and, very rarely, it's the drummer. In some groups, *all* members sing. But there's always at least one; someone's got to do it. There's indeed a microphone on a short stand in the back, next to a Marshall amp, but this is ignored as the band begins to play.

Drummer Damon Che kicks things off by repeatedly smashing his open high-hat. The guitarist, Ian Williams, soon accompanies him, plucking single notes seemingly at random. The tone is clean and bright. Bassist Eric Emm, playing a Fender and wearing a button-down shirt with sleeves rolled up to his elbows, joins in next. Rather than lock in with the drums, Emm also plays notes that simultaneously sound arbitrary and yet like they belong.

Williams, donning a plain white T-shirt, plays with his black Gibson hung unfashionably high on his chest. It's probably six inches from his face. Most rock guitarists play their instruments as low as possible. Peter Hook, bassist for Joy Division and New Order, performs with his instrument practically scraping the stage. Halfway through the song, Williams places the pick in his teeth so he can use the fingers on his strumming hand to frenetically tap out notes on the strings. His left hand, meanwhile, continues to spider across the fretboard. All eight fingers fill the room with a brilliant and seemingly irregular array of spiky notes. It's a technique that made Eddie Van Halen famous, not that any of this sounds remotely like Van Halen. Williams chews gum while he plays, occasionally blowing pink bubbles.

After the song ends, Che reaches for the microphone on the short stand. "Ah, sweet Chicago," he says, "thank you." Over the course of the night, Don Cab will play ten songs. None of them feature lyrics or singing of any kind. Che's the only member of the band to address the crowd, not that he says much. What's there to say?

The next song is as fast and frenetic as the first. While both guitarists are amazing players (even Emm can tap), Che is the real star of the show. He pounds away on a black Pearl Export, the cheapest Pearl set you can buy. The huge floor toms are high and flat, a look inspired by Earl Hudson of Bad Brains. The cymbals are also high but tilted. Except for the high hat, they're all rides, even though he swats at them like a crash. The cymbal he hits the most, a Sabian B8 Pro, has a super resonant bell; when he hits it with the butt end of the thick marching band sticks, it resembles a huge, clanging church bell. A maple Ludwig snare is low and set at an odd angle; Che's hands must drop to well below his knees to hit it. On his right, next to one of the floor toms, there's a piccolo snare that he uses to get in timbale licks.

Che's a big guy, at least six foot five. Despite having had the flu for a month, his long arms move in a whirlwind around the kit. On the band's most recent record, he's credited simply as Octopus. It's easy to tell why. Arms and sticks flail in all directions, producing sound that is both adroit and chaotic. Che's feet are just as quick. His right foot pumps up and down like a jackrabbit's. But it's not just about speed. He's a hard hitter. When he makes a rimshot, it sounds like a gunshot. Before the show he nailed his bass drum to the floor to keep it from moving forward. It's a trick he learned from jazz drummer Elvin Jones. In a dive like the Fireside, the owner doesn't mind yet another hole in the floor. When the band plays nicer clubs, the practice is frowned upon.

When the song ends to hearty applause, Che reaches again for the microphone. "I don't know what it is about the Fireside Bowl," he says, out of breath, "but this is a lot of fun."

Not originally a local act—Don Caballero formed in Pittsburgh in 1991, released its first record in 1993—the band has since moved to Chicago. It's a good home base. Their label, Touch and Go, is here. There are several clubs where they can draw a good audience most nights of the week, not to mention the city is home to a few like-minded bands that play music that's somewhat similar.

This is already Don Cab's third Chicago show just this year. In November, they'll play yet another, at the Lounge Ax. They'd been playing there ever since becoming a band, and they always look forward to it. The owners, Sue and Julia, treat groups with respect and there's always a good crowd. Local legend Wesley Willis, a musician and artist living with schizophrenia who releases album after album of nursery rhyme-like songs shouted over pre-programmed keyboard beats, even wrote a song about them playing there. The song's chorus consists of nothing but Willis screaming out the group's name over and over. In his idiosyncratic howl, it comes out, "Don Cab-A-larow!"

The band's touring behind its third album, *What Burns Never Returns*, released in June the previous year. Even though the LP has only eight tracks, on vinyl it's a double record. Two songs per side. Most of the tracks are long; none are under four minutes. The opening song is almost ten minutes. The titles, just like on previous records, are lengthy and somewhat nonsensical: "Delivering The Groceries At 138 Beats Per Minute," "Slice Where You Live Like Pie." The cover is a haunting photograph of a house bathed in a green glow with a column of lights behind it. What's happening in the picture? Are aliens invading? Is it the end of the world? In the eighties there'd been all that talk of nuclear annihilation and acid rain. Is that what we're looking at? A year later American Football's debut record would look awfully similar. Like most things, Don Caballero got there first.

They've been playing shows sporadically since *What Burns* came out, going on short tours or playing around Chicago.

In fact, their first show of 1999 was here at the Fireside Bowl in January, a warm-up gig before heading to Europe for a handful of dates. Back then, the group had been a four piece, with Mike Banfield on guitar in addition to Ian Williams. Banfield had been one of the original members from nearly a decade before, but he left after the shows in Europe, when the group decided to move to Chicago. He had a day job he liked in Pittsburgh and didn't want to give it up, so he gave up the band instead.

Pat Morris, the original bassist who'd been with Don Cab since the beginning—and who'd played on *What Burns*—was next to leave. He was replaced by Eric Emm. Emm played bass in Williams's other band, Storm and Stress, an experimental rock trio also signed to Touch and Go. In that band, in addition to playing guitar, Williams sang. Not to be outdone, Damon Che (full name Damon Che Fitzgerald; he dropped Fitzgerald to avoid confusion with his father, a well-known local musician) has another group too. Thee (or The) Speaking Canaries have released three records. Che plays guitar and sings. The guys onstage tonight—Che, Williams, and Emm—will later be considered the classic Don Caballero lineup. Too bad it won't last long. The band will break up within a year.

Going from a quartet to a trio didn't slow them down. Even live they still have a huge and full sound. Both Emm and Williams use looping pedals to stack guitar lines, riffs one on top of the other. Despite there only being one guitarist and bassist on stage, the audience is hearing half a dozen different parts. Accompanying all that sound isn't a problem for Che; he already sounds like at least two people.

The structure of the songs is hard to pick out. They don't follow the usual verse-chorus-verse format. Instead, one section transitions quickly to another and then another. By the time a listener has a chance to lock into any sort of recognizable or repeated melody, the tune quickly shifts to something else. At times, it even sounds like each of the three band members is playing a different song. Emm hits notes that don't seem to match what Williams is plucking or tapping, while the insane fills and rolls produced by Che at first appear to have no relation to the rhythm or melody being produced by the guitars. But it works. It all coheres into a whole that somehow makes sense. Not that the crowd know what to do with what they're hearing. A few try to move or bob their heads to the beat, but with the beat and rhythm constantly changing, that's hard to do. On the black awning outside the club they'd played last night, it says MUSIC FRIENDLY DANCE. The crowd tonight at the Fireside Bowl don't do a lot of dancing; it's not necessarily the kind the music you can move to.

As the concert goes on, Don Cab does the usual things in between songs: they tune up, take a swig of beer, wipe sweat from their faces with a towel. Che uses the mike to repeatedly thank the audience. At the end of the show, after an hour of playing, the crowd claps and cheers. Che give a final thanks and the band leaves the stage. But what just happened? What kind of music was that? Where did it come from, and how you do you play it? And, perhaps most important of all, what do you call it?

1   All Is Number: What Is Math Rock?

I should mention at the very beginning that math rock bands all have different opinions of and relationships to the term. Most musicians, like Don Caballero's Ian Williams and Damon Che, warily accept it, resigned to the fact that the name is the name and there's not much that can be done about it now. "I'm sort of at the 'I don't really care anymore' stage," says Williams. "On a certain level I've given up." Che agrees. "If it sticks it sticks, there's nothing you can do about it. It's like a nickname." Piglet's Matthew Parrish has learned to just shrug his shoulders at the label. "I don't really take any terms to identify sub-categorization very seriously and, if I use them, it's usually tongue-in-cheek." Sam Weatherald, from Clever Girl, sees logic in the name. "I think it does indicate a certain focus on precise compositional complexity and unusual time signatures, which certainly is pretty descriptive of some bands like Don Caballero, so it makes sense as a genre, yeah." Many musicians are generally indifferent ("I am neither for nor against the term 'math rock,'" says Pretend's Luke Palascak), or else just hoped for something with a bit more oomph ("I don't think 'math rock' sounds cool," says Drew Fitchette from Rooftops, "I wish it sounded more kickass than it does").

Some musicians aren't too keen on term. "I really don't like it," says Gregor Fair from Foster Parents. "It feels cold and clinical and, when used alone, it's not always representative of the music seeing as so much is lumped with the tag." Others feel more strongly than that. "I hate the term 'math rock,' I cannot stand it," John Stanier told *Drummers Journal* in 2015. Stanier drummed for nineties alternative metal band Helmet and is currently in the math rock adjacent group Battles alongside Ian Williams. "I think it's disgusting, I think it's dismissive. It's unsexy, it's really gross."

Why all the pushback? I suppose it's because people don't like to be pigeonholed, put into boxes, or have their artistic ambitions reduced to a pat two-word description (especially one they didn't choose). Musicians consider themselves to be big thinkers, and any attempt to pin them down just makes them feel small. In their protests you can hear the cry of Walt Whitman: "I am large, I contain multitudes." So then why am I intent on discussing decades of music, hundreds of bands, and thousands of songs in the context of a category that many of the prime creators of that very music hold in disdain? Because to talk about anything, you first need to name it. And the more musical styles that come into existence, the more terms we need to invent to refer to them. This means that any genre tag, math rock included, isn't meant to limit, judge, or denigrate, but rather is just to define and contain for the purposes of examination.

The fact that the term "math rock" started as a joke is probably one of the reasons why bands don't like it. As guitarist Matt Sweeney, from the nineties indie rock group Chavez, told *Pitchfork* in 2006:

> It was invented by a friend of ours as a derogatory term for a band me and James [Lo, Chavez's drummer] played in called Wider. But his whole joke is that he'd watch the song and not react at all, and then take out his calculator to figure out how good the song was.

So he'd call it math rock, and it was a total diss, as it should be.

Would it have helped if the term originated in a less offhand manner? Would musicians then take it more seriously? Probably not. The term post-rock (a genre which has considerable overlap with math rock, a topic I'll discuss in Chapter 4) was coined by the well-respected author and music journalist Simon Reynolds. It first appeared in the pages of the esteemed magazine *The Wire*, and bands still hated it.

Whether or not the name math rock was born as a goof or a diss doesn't necessarily mean it has no meaning or validity. At a certain point, music indeed comes down to math, and numbers are crucial if not inherent to the form. Scholars and thinkers have been using math to talk and think about music for thousands of years. It started with the influential Greek philosopher Pythagoras who, as far back as 500 BC, was mapping harmonies to mathematical calculations. "Pythagoras's attempt to define and constrain musical sounds by use of numbers and ratios continues to shape how we conceptualize and perform songs in the current day, and even how we distinguish between melody and noise," writes Ted Gioia in his 2019 book *Music: A Subversive History*.

Pythagoras was just the beginning. Later academics and intellectuals would similarly base both an appreciation and a framework around music's relationship to math (or vice versa). In a 1712 letter to fellow mathematician Christian Goldbach, Gottfried Leibniz wrote, "Music is the pleasure the human mind experiences from counting without being aware that it is counting." For millennia, music and math were seen as two sides of the same coin. However, over time the disciplines and interests of art and science began to diverge. "Today we think in terms of math/science people or verbal/artistic people.

There's that division, "Wayne Parker, a senior researcher at Johns Hopkins University told *Johns Hopkins Magazine* in 1998. "In the past, math, music, and reading held the liberal arts together."

I suspect that this idea of a division between math people and artistic people forms the bedrock of the resistance musicians have to their work being labeled "math rock." It's antithetical to how they see themselves (namely, as artists) not to mention it appears in their minds as something oxymoronic, a bizarre creation, some sort of clockwork orange (the mechanical masquerading as organic). *Math* has the connotation of being coldly clinical, the stuff of nerds and geeks. *Rock,* meanwhile, is wild and uninhibited, always and forever cool and rebellious. Putting those two things together, as John Stanier says, is "gross," a bizarre and unpalatable combination not unlike the scoop of spaghetti sitting on top of a hot dog that adorns the cover of "The Yabba," a single by Battles.

But as much as Stanier and others wish or try to separate their work from the science and intellectual rigor of math, it's not going to happen. In an article published in *The Guardian* in 2011, British mathematician Marcus du Sautoy wrote, "Rhythm depends on arithmetic, harmony draws from basic numerical relationships, and the development of musical themes reflects the world of symmetry and geometry." In the same article from *Johns Hopkins Magazine* quoted above, math professor (and amateur musician) Dan Naiman says, "In jazz, especially, you look for patterns that have a mathematical structure—the repetition, the way you put it together, the exercises are very mathematical." Even a notoriously bare-bones band such as The Ramones famously began their tunes with bassist Dee Dee Ramone shouting out "1-2-3-4!" You simply can't play music without numbers and, when you're dealing with a whole lot of numbers, they inevitably turn into math.

In the end, it doesn't matter what we call any style music (to paraphrase another poet, an English one this time, "a genre by any other name would sound as sweet"). The important thing is to discuss and celebrate the records and songs and musicians who created the music. That's the aim and goal of this book.

●

Let me pause for a moment to describe, if not wholly define, the term; to echo Raymond Carver, What do we talk about when we talk about math rock?

Math rock is a largely instrumental genre consisting of elements from free jazz, prog, and hardcore (I'll discuss these influences more in Chapter 2). Math rock groups are usually constrained to drums, guitar, and bass. Math rock songs are often long and feature just the few instruments already mentioned. You may hear a keyboard flourish here or there, or the occasional wash of electronics, but mostly what you hear in math rock is the sound of a band in a room whaling away on instruments. That's it. Math rock bands don't pair themselves up with a symphony or hire choirs to provide backing vocals. You're also not going to see tons of members in a math rock band. Several groups, like Hella, Giraffes? Giraffes! and Standards, are just a duo of guitar and drums. Here and there groups swell to five members, and a lot are quartets, but trios seem to be the sweet spot in terms of personnel. Why? Because guitar, bass, and drums are math rock's main musical ingredients.

The sound of math rock is structured mayhem, at once organized and messy. It's played with NASA-like precision by musicians who are blindingly and almost mystically adept at their instruments. Fingers dance over guitar necks, drummers pound out polyrhythms in 13/8 time, and singers often need not apply, because the music doesn't have the space or need for words. (Speaking of singers, most of this book will look at instrumental math rock since I consider that to be the purest form of the genre.) Instead of radio-friendly pop music you get long, complex tracks filled with crystalline electric guitar, explosive drumming, and dozens of musical ideas. That's not to say it's solely for music-snobs or intellectuals. The best math rock hits you in two places at once: the head and the gut. And just because the odd and always-changing time signatures make it hard to dance to, that doesn't mean math rock won't make you *feel*. Its songs can be deeply emotional, containing highs and lows and eliciting laughter or tears, no mean feat for a largely instrumental form. Math rock also doesn't take itself too seriously. Looking at a few titles of math rock songs ("Am I Just a Bunch of Particles That Thinks It's a Bunch of Particles?" by Zoo Strategies or "When The Catholic Girls Go Camping, The Nicotine Vampires Rule Supreme" by Giraffes? Giraffes!) proves these bands have a sense of humor in addition to serious chops.

Math rock, which was born in the nineties just as the internet was becoming prevalent, is also the perfect genre for our completely digital and connected age. Playlists and tutorials on YouTube collectively rack up millions of views, while platforms like Spotify and Bandcamp create new fans every day. But the web does more than just spread the word. The fractured and maximalist sensibility of the genre is the perfect musical accompaniment to a world where attention has been atomized and millennia of information is only a tap away. As a commenter on Reddit put it, math rock "literally sounds like my own thinking patterns in music form."

The main appeal of math rock is that it's *music* music. It's highly technical stuff you can dig your sonic teeth into.

Take something like "Don Caballero 3" from Don Cab's *What Burns Never Returns*. The song is nearly ten minutes of aural experiments, surprises, and jagged edges. The drumming is off kilter, changing every couple of bars, and the guitars percolate rather than deliver power chords. The track is a rollercoaster ride whooshing up and down and taking turn after turn; by the end, you're wrung out but kind of want to ride it again.

Beyond just the aggressiveness with which the music is sometimes played, math rock's instrumental nature gives the genre an added dimension. Listening to a song with a stated story or narrative is an almost totally passive experience. You're just sitting there taking in what the band gives you. But when you listen to an instrumental song that refuses to provide any sort of center, or stated subject matter, it leaves you free to think critically about what you're hearing. You can make up your own mind in terms of what the song is or might be about. Math rock draws you in and makes you an active participant.

That doesn't mean it's easy. Being a hardcore fan of the genre can mean looking at songs in an analytical and sometimes numerical manner. You won't be asked to get out a pen and paper, but listening to certain bands will feel at times like homework. If that sounds like a turn off, that's fine. You can always just play Daft Punk's *Homework* instead. No one will judge you. But if you choose to put in the work and delve into the various musical strands and logistical webs of what the best of math rock represents, you'll be rewarded with an audio experience that is at once wholly emotionally and intellectually gratifying. It is, in my view, the most mind-expanding and soul satisfying music made in the last fifty years.

My approach in the ensuing pages is not to tell the chronological story of math rock. The reason for this is simple: that story can't be told. It doesn't exist. Whereas some genres are synonymous with a particular group or era (Sex Pistols and punk, Nirvana and grunge, Happy Mondays and Madchester), math rock is bigger than one band, one era, one town, or one scene. There's just no singular hub around which all the spokes are attached. There's also no undisputed pinnacle or acknowledged heyday, an either commercial or artistic peak that's never been equaled. This is a good thing. It means that math rock remains a vibrant and living form, always looking forward and rarely looking back. Today there are math rock bands all over the world (in addition to math rock websites, music festivals, and record labels), and all of them are dedicated to pushing the genre in new directions and to new heights. So instead of presenting events in order and stating merely that this band led to that band, what I've done is break the genre down to its constituent parts. Chapters delve into subjects like how math rock is played, how the songs are written, and where the form came from. The result is less a history of the scene than a biography of the sound.

You may read this book straight through if you wish, or you can skip around using the table of contents as your guide. You can also just flip to a passage or section or paragraph at random and start reading. Math rock is nonlinear, discursive, and unexpected. Your experience reading *Math Rock* can be the same. The choice is yours.

2 Breadcrumb Trail: The Origins of Math Rock

Novelist Cormac McCarthy told the *New York Times* in 1992, "The ugly fact is books are made out of books." The same goes for music. Genres are a Frankenstein's monster constructed from a variety of bands, songs, styles, and traditions that often go back decades. Detecting these roots, and putting together that story, is not always easy. "Musical movements don't begin suddenly," wrote Hank Shteamer in *Rolling Stone* in 2019, "they take shape slowly, their origins defined only in hindsight." Now that we're thirty years removed from the naming of math rock, we indeed have the requisite perspective with which to document the genre's origins.

Math rock was created primarily from three sources: free jazz, prog rock, and hardcore/thrash metal. Other musical strands of course fed into the form, and individual math rock players all undoubtedly found inspiration outside of these three scenes, but these were the main musical movements that laid the groundwork for math rock. We'll look at each of them in chronological order.

After reigning as the most creative American artform, and the most exciting thing happening in music for decades, by the fifties jazz had settled into a general format and routine. Live, and on record, almost all jazz followed a similar template. Musicians would begin by playing a melody or general harmonic theme. The players would then improvise, with various members of the band taking solos before returning to the main melody and finishing the song. Tunes usually lasted for thirty-two bars, with four beats in each bar (shorter songs might only feature sixteen or just twelve bars). Rhythmically, almost all jazz was in 4/4 time, meaning there were four beats to the bar. Most pop music, from this period and beyond, continues to be in 4/4; it's so ubiquitous it's also known as "common time," because it's so commonly used.

By 1959, things were beginning to change. This watershed year saw the appearance of several groundbreaking jazz LPs, some of which would prove wildly popular, while others were hugely influential (and one was both). In just twelve months, *Time Out* by The Dave Brubeck Quartet, *Mingus Ah Um* by Charles Mingus, *The Shape of Jazz to Come* by Ornette Coleman, John Coltrane's *Giant Steps*, and *Kind of Blue* by Miles Davis were all released. Each of them was revolutionary in its own way. Mingus's record was fiercely political, while *The Shape of Jazz to Come*, Coleman's third record (but first for Atlantic), pointed toward where the form was headed. *Kind of Blue* would go on to become the bestselling jazz album of all time, while *Time Out* introduced the idea of odd time signatures into the lexicon of not only jazz but popular music.

Time Out, where each song was played in a different and sometimes exotic time signature, was Brubeck's way of breaking jazz out of a rut. "Should some cool-minded Martian come to earth and check on the state of our music," Brubeck wrote in *Take Five's* liner notes, "he might play through 10,000 jazz records before he found one that wasn't in common 4/4 time." The track "Take Five" was in 5/4, while opening tune "Blue Rondo A La Turk" was in 9/8, grouped 2-2-2-3 (a common rhythm in Turkish music, hence "Turk" in the title; Brubeck had heard it on the streets of Istanbul). *Take Five* was at first considered a dud and didn't initially meet with much success. The LP was out for a year before Columbia's president, Goddard Lieberson, decided to release the title track as a single. To everyone's astonishment, it went to #1. It's remained a jazz staple ever since, influencing countless musicians. Even slacker band Pavement, on their second album, 1994's *Crooked Rain, Crooked Rain*, included a sort of homage/parody entitled "5-4=Unity." Math rock's penchant for odd time signatures no doubt has some roots in *Take Five*.

A year after Brubeck's audacious but ultimately successful experiment was a hit, Ornette Coleman pushed jazz even further with the release of his 1961 album *Free Jazz*. Even though the band featured eight players, rather than listing the artist as the Ornette Coleman Octet, the LP is credited to the Ornette Coleman Double Quartet. The reason for this is *Free Jazz* features one long piece, broken up into two sides, played by two four-piece bands performing at the same time. It was recorded in one continuous take; there were no overdubs, splices, or editing. Side 2 picks up right where Side 1 quickly fades out. Each quartet contained a reed, trumpet, bass, and drums, and all eight players are playing and improvising at the same time (with each quartet panned to a different stereo channel; listening to the LP with headphones on is like hearing two different records simultaneously). The music, however, wasn't completely spontaneous. Some pre-arranged transitional cues were given to the players to introduce their individual solos, each of which lasts about five minutes, apart from Coleman's which lasts for ten (picking out these written passages from the rest of the cacophony, however, is like playing a musical version of *Where's Waldo*). Coleman's aim was for the music to be direct and immediate, with no pre-conceived chord patterns or tired musical clichés. The result is a mind-blowing swirling storm of sound.

The record spawned the new genre of free jazz, with players all over the world taking up Coleman's challenge and leaving behind jazz's (and Western music's) long-held traditions and views around melody, harmony, and structure. Free jazz was almost always challenging, abrasive, and atonal. It was also divisive. When *Free Jazz* was first released, the premier jazz magazine *Downbeat* issued two reviews for the album. One critic gave it five stars (out of five). The other gave it zero.

The cover of *Free Jazz* features Jackson Pollock's 1954 painting "White Light." Pollock was a painter who eschewed the materials and tools of classical artists. Instead of watercolors or oils, he used house paint. In place of delicate brushes or an easel, he rolled out his canvases on the floor and used wooden sticks. For "White Light" he squeezed paint onto the canvas directly from the tubes. It was one of the last works he ever made, and it was the only one he produced that year. In 1955 Pollock gave up painting; the following year he died in a drunken car accident. Beyond being just one nonconformist acknowledging another, Coleman's use of "White Light" was intended to give listeners a clue about the music found inside. Pollock was an abstract painter; Coleman was creating abstract music. You might even say that the chaotic and energetic *Free Jazz* was the musical equivalent of Pollock's frenzied and buzzing canvas. But there was something else beyond this surface comparison. The abstraction in these works gave their creators freedom. Pollock was a painter who ventured into the unknown and did exactly what he wanted. Coleman was following his lead. They each wanted to release themselves from the confines of their chosen medium; abstraction allowed them to do it.

In the same way Ornette Coleman was inspired by Jackson Pollock's maverick abstract aesthetic, math rock was similarly inspired by *Free Jazz*. "Math rock's not music that's interested in a main vocal melody line," says Theo Cateforis, an author and professor with a Ph.D. in Music History. "It's not going to give you a verse or a chorus. It's not to going give you those types of things. You're going to get riffs, certainly, that repeat and that you'll recognize, but it's going to be a lot more abstract in nature."

If you listen to *Free Jazz* next to records by Don Caballero or Toe, it may be hard to hear the connection between the genre that grew out of Coleman's record and where math rock ended up thirty years later. Ornette Coleman's double quartets are playing what sounds like mostly chaos, whereas math rock bands—even at their most harsh—are playing music with identifiable notes within some sort of arrangement, as scattered or seemingly nonsensical as it may seem to be. But it's the freedom, along with the general complexity of approach, that math rock took from Coleman and the others. In the liner notes of *The Shape of Jazz to Come*, Coleman's stunning record from 1959 (and the opening salvo of a conversation he would kick off in earnest with *Free Jazz*), Martin Williams of *The Jazz Review* wrote, "His musical inspiration operates in a world uncluttered by conventional bar lines, conventional chord changes, and conventional ways of blowing or fingering a saxophone." Coleman was all about leaving legacy behind and creating something new. Math rock bands followed suit, embracing abstraction, and leaving behind traditional or typical song structures.

•

While Jazz has been seen for more than a century as the embodiment of cool, progressive rock was pretty much always the opposite. Even at the height of its brief spasm of popularity in the early seventies, when prog bands like Yes, Genesis, Jethro Tull, and Emerson, Lake and Palmer were filling arenas and selling millions of albums, "cool" would not have been the word to describe the scene or the bands (e.g., ELP's second album, *Tarkus,* features a giant armadillo tank on the cover). After punk did its best to kill off prog, the genre limped along, wounded but not entirely defeated. As the years went by, there were fewer and fewer prog bands and, of the ones that remained, many changed their sound (and their look) to fit in with the era of MTV. Sometimes this worked and they had hits (Genesis was an eighties juggernaut), but most often they didn't. As time went on, something unexpected began to happen. The prog sound—characterized as "high degrees of instrumental and compositional complexity" by Paul Stump in his book *The Music's All That Matters*—began to show up in all kinds of unexpected places. More and more modern groups were producing music that was unmistakably prog. The genre that had supposedly been dealt a deathblow by Johnny Rotten's infamous "I Hate Pink Floyd" T-shirt was back (not that it had ever left).

Like so many innovations in pop music over the past fifty years, it all started with The Beatles. The band's 1967 masterpiece *Sgt. Pepper's Lonely Hearts Club Band* proved that the album format could be an artistic statement. Pop songs could now be kaleidoscopic, trippy, adventurous. By the end of the sixties, sonically adventurous bands weren't content to just don a kaftan and incorporate a strange instrument or two. They wanted to go even farther, experimenting with time signatures, and taking rock to the absolute outer limits in terms of subject matter, length, and sound. A band who helped lead the way was one who had been a darling of the psychedelic rock scene (and, later, punk's number one enemy),

Pink Floyd. As Will Romano writes in his book *Close to the Edge: How Yes's Masterpiece Defined Prog Rock*, "Floyd created the bridge between psychedelia and progressive with 'Echoes' from 1971's *Meddle*." That track—composed by all four group members and clocking in at over twenty-three minutes—includes sound effects, musical improvisation, and lengthy instrumental passages, touchstones which would all (for better or worse) be associated with prog.

In their quest to reject musical clichés and avoid predictable patterns, prog bands renounced almost all forms of American music. Blues licks were out, as was any sort of influence from R&B or country music. This was a crucial and major break from the preexisting rock scene, which had spent the sixties fervently mining this territory (The Rolling Stones owed their entire career to American blues). Instead, groups looked to the European tradition of classical music (ELP didn't even consider themselves a "rock band," seeing as how they played adaptations of classical pieces such as "Pictures at an Exhibition" by Mussorgsky). Prog songs soon began to resemble the composition of classical pieces; they were long and contained extended structures and repeated motifs. Whereas the psychedelic bands often played long improvised passages (The Grateful Dead made a whole career out of it), prog bands sought to contain the sonic experimentation of the psyche scene within the framework and shape of classical music. Rock, it was said, had gone to college. This was "thinking man's music."

It was interesting and exciting stuff. And yet, even in its heyday, many were skeptical at what was seen as prog's inherent pretentiousness. In *A New Day Yesterday: UK Progressive Rock and the 1970s*, Mike Barnes wrote that "'self-indulgence' was a term that was prevalent in the music press, although it was almost always used pejoratively by the back-to-basics brigade. But if one looks at it from a different angle, it can just as easily be synonymous with risk taking, experimentation, boundary-pushing and unfettered self-expression—doing exactly what one wants."

There absolutely was a great deal of excess in prog: side-long epics, concept records, twenty-minute organ solos. Some of that was indeed indulgent if not plain silly (songs about fairies and trolls; Rick Wakeman playing eight keyboards while sporting not only a cape but a wizard's hat), but it was all born out of the freedom that Barnes describes. Sometimes that meant Robert Fripp playing his electric guitar sitting on a stool because that's how he felt most comfortable, and sometimes that meant a double record with only four songs inspired by a footnote in Paramahansa Yogananda's *Autobiography of a Yogi* (give *Tales from Topographic Oceans* a chance; it's amazing). But what often gets lost in the debate over prog being indulgent or excessive is just how good and ambitious almost all of it was. Whether it was in lyrical content, technical prowess, or state of the art recording techniques, the prog scene of the seventies was a masterclass in pushing boundaries and trying to reach new heights. Not that many people admitted it.

Radiohead, after the release of *OK Computer*, were asked by reporters whether prog was an influence, to which they quickly replied, "No. We all *hate* progressive rock music." And yet the six-and-a half-minute lead single "Paranoid Android"— with its various segments and shifts in mood, tempo, and instrumentation—follows the prog format to a T. The band's being disingenuous, if not just plain dishonest, to deny prog as an influence.

Despite Radiohead's protests, prog's fingerprints are all over nineties indie rock. For example, the title track off the 1974 album *Red* by King Crimson sounds exactly like Steve Albini's band Shellac (or rather, whole swathes of Shellac sound just like King Crimson). If that song had been a single on Touch and Go in 1992, Chicago hipsters would have absolutely loved it. A whole lot of the second-wave post-rock scene—bands like Slint and Sigur Rós—could accurately be described as neo-prog. Today, there are several adventurous, noisy, and fearless bands—such as Black Midi, Squid, Caroline, and Black Country, New Road—who are all carrying forward many of the musical traits prog championed.

Among the many similarities that math rock shares with prog is that a math rock song can (and will) go anywhere. It'll shift in sound and tempo and instrumentation, abruptly stopping or curving in unexpected directions. The same goes for prog. In his foreword to *Wonderous Stories: A Journey Through the Landscape of Progressive Rock*, Genesis guitarist Steve Hackett writes, "Prog has always had the element of surprise on its side. Like a film for the ear, you never know what scene is going to unfold next." What both prog and math rock do is keep the listener unsettled and on edge; each track is its own world of mystery and suspense.

Structurally, there's also a lot of prog in math rock. The genre's long songs with complicated structures, shifting tempos, and difficult time signatures are right out of the prog handbook. I also think the basic essence of what prog exemplified—pushing boundaries and carrying music forward—is exactly what math rock bands stand for. In the seventies, if you just wanted to bang out three chord songs, you formed a pub rock band. If you wanted to do the same thing in the nineties, you moved to Seattle and aped Nirvana. In the seventies, if you wanted to take music to a new place, you played prog. In the nineties and beyond, to do the same thing, you'd play math rock.

•

Today Metallica is considered one of the most successful groups of all time. They've won nine Grammys, sold more than a hundred million records, and routinely play to sold-out crowds in arenas all over the world. But their career got off to a rough start. On the band's first release, as part of a 1982 compilation called *Metal Massacre*, their name was misspelled as *Mettallica*. At the time, the band wasn't much of a band. Based in Los Angeles, they'd formed in 1981 around the nucleus of drummer Lars Ulrich and guitarist and singer James Hetfield. Their contribution to *Metal Massacre*, "Hit the Lights," featured just Ulrich and Hetfield, along with a guitar solo from their friend Lloyd Grant who occasionally played with the band. The song itself was a holdover from Hetfield's previous group, Leather Charm. When Metallica had made their live debut that March in Anaheim, their set was mostly covers and the small crowd didn't know what to make of them. Metallica were modeling themselves after a bunch of British bands, led by Judas Priest and Iron Maiden, who had been dubbed in 1979 the New Wave of British Heavy Metal by *Sounds* writer Geoff Barton (the moniker was often shortened to the useful but unsightly acronym NWOBHM). Metallica loved the NWOBHM bands but wanted to push metal even further. As a new and struggling group, they didn't quite have the chops, or the gear, to play heavier or louder than their heroes, but they were able to best them in one area: speed.

Of the ten acts featured on *Metal Massacre*, most were local bands, like Octave, Bitch, and Demon Flight. They'd each played around town, released a few things on small regional labels, and eventually broke up. Another one of the groups, Ratt, would soon soften their sound and join acts like Mötley Crüe in the hair metal/glam revival that was kicking off in Los Angeles. (Two years after *Metal Massacre* came out, Ratt scored a top forty hit with "Round and Round.") Metallica didn't want to just play small clubs, and they didn't want to peddle any sort of watered-down pop music version of hard rock. They wanted to play the gnarliest, meanest, and most aggressive form of heavy metal. They had some company. Slayer, also just getting started around LA, along with Exodus in the Bay Area, and Anthrax and Overkill on the East Coast were each developing a new and faster form of metal that came to be known as thrash.

Malcolm Dome coined the term in *Kerrang!* using Anthrax's "Metal Thrashing Mad" as the inspiration. Thrash bands took the speed and intensity of hardcore and married it with the sound and imagery of the NWOBHM groups. At first, it was a tough sell. The heaviness of the music, along with graphic lyrics that went far beyond what mainstream metal bands were singing about, kept the scene underground. Thrash bands couldn't get their music distributed, let alone on the radio. Instead, groups relied on zines, a distribution network of tiny independent labels, and hand-dubbed cassettes rabidly traded by fans.

Thrash, while sticking closely to the usual heavy metal tropes of palm-muted chugging and dazzling solos, also contained something new and exciting: precision. "A lot of thrash metal isn't really thrashing madly about," says Simon Reynolds, author of *Rip It Up and Start Again* and *Retromania*. "It's very, very controlled but also very fast and intricate."

Metallica and Anthrax were taking the framework of heavy metal, grafting onto it the speed of hardcore, and combining both with a new exploration of complex parts and tempo shifts. Songs often stretched to six or eight minutes, and some were instrumental. Much of it wasn't too far off from what math rock or mathcore would later become. And while it may seem strange to speak of Metallica and math rock in the same sentence, in the early eighties the lines between genres weren't so clearly defined.

The recording of Metallica's demo, which later became known as *No Life 'Til Leather*, was paid for by Kenny Kaye from High Velocity Records. High Velocity was an Orange County punk label who'd released singles by ska band Din and Norm Norman, a new wave singer who made a minor splash with the song "You're a Zombie." Kaye booked Metallica into the same studio in East Tustin where hardcore band Lost Cause had recorded their "Born Dead" seven inch. Kaye was shocked when he heard Metallica's original material (including a much tighter version of "Hit the Lights"; by now future Megadeth vocalist Dave Mustaine was in the band on lead guitar). It turned out the songs Kaye had liked live were by seventies British band Diamond Head. When Kaye passed on the group, Metallica released the cassette themselves. Friends and record stores dubbed copies for would-be fans all over the country. It worked. Despite not making much noise on the competitive LA scene, when Metallica played in northern California, it was a very different story. The crowds loved them and sang along to every song. The band decided to move to San Francisco.

Just as Metallica was heading north, another group from southern California was also looking to transform the strident sound of hardcore into something new. Hermosa Beach's Black Flag was busy taking the blueprint of hardcore punk—a template largely created by Black Flag's guitarist and founder Greg Ginn—and pushing it to new extremes.

Hardcore scenes had been bubbling up all over the country since the late seventies. Washington, DC, and New York had each seen an explosion of new and interesting bands, but Black Flag had pretty much been the first. Formed way back in 1976, Black Flag—through its incessant guerilla touring—had cobbled together practically from scratch a cross-country network of clubs and venues where punk and hardcore bands could face friendly audiences. Ginn's SST Records was also a hugely influential presence on the scene, putting out—in addition to albums from his own band—records by The Minutemen, Hüsker Dü, Stains, Subhumans, and Meat Puppets.

Ginn had been pushing both Black Flag's sound and image ever since the beginning. Just as hardcore was solidifying into a singular, and somewhat stultifying, musical style consisting of short, fast, and politically tinged songs, Black Flag tunes became longer, slower, and more opaque. And at a time when the East Coast Straight Edge kids were shaving their heads and signing on to an ascetic lifestyle free of drink and drugs, Ginn and his Black Flag bandmates grew out their hair and extolled the virtues of pot. The band's most provocative act was the instrumental record *The Process of Weeding Out*, released in the fall of 1985. A four song EP clocking in at just under a half hour, it was tracked at a marathon recording session in March that yielded enough material for *Weeding Out* and the two full-length LPs from that year, *Loose Nut* and *In My Head*.

In Stevie Chick's history of the band, *Spray Paint the Walls*, he describes Black Flag's instrumental tracks as "darkly inventive, seethingly ferocious jamming." The improvisational, jazz-punk vibe was wildly at odds with the primal punk the band had previously performed. As drummer Bill Stevenson told Jim Ruland for his history of SST records, *Corporate Rock Sucks,* "We were playing stuff that was more like Ornette Coleman, or things that were more like Charlie Parker or things that were more like the Mahavishnu Orchestra or King Crimson or Sabbath."

Greg Ginn was a huge fan of jazz and especially John McLaughlin's fusion group Mahavishnu Orchestra, who he'd seen live many times. McLaughlin was a skilled and inventive guitarist who'd played with Miles Davis (including on the landmark LP *Bitches Brew*, the album that kickstarted the rock-jazz-fusion movement). McLaughlin struck out on his own in the early seventies, forming Mahavishnu Orchestra out of his love of jazz, rock, and Indian classical music. The band excelled at playing complicated guitar-based instrumental music that often contained unusual time signatures. Today, a lot of it sounds like a primitive version of math rock (check out the band's first album, *The Inner Mounting Flame*). Hermosa Beach also happened to be home to a legendary jazz club called The Lighthouse, where Ginn saw dozens of jazz greats play over the years.

The Process of Weeding Out found the band winning praise from the most unlikely of sources: the *New York Times*. Writing a few months after the EP came out in a 1986 article entitled "Black Flag Adds a Soupcon of Sophistication to Punk Rock," Robert Palmer favorably compared the songs to Ornette Coleman and Eastern music. "As the piece picks up steam, the three musicians weave the original thematic threads into its onrushing momentum. The end result is an exciting, genre-stretching performance with an overall direction, coherence and unity."

Not everyone was thrilled with the band's new direction, something Ginn saw coming. In fact, he had intended from the beginning for the EP to alienate his audience (the title is a double pun; he wanted to "weed out" the band's more casual fans, and he was also heavily into smoking marijuana at the time). It worked. Many of Black Flag's longtime listeners didn't know what to make of the record, especially since it came after the almost equally divisive LP from the previous year, *My War*, whose second side strayed awfully far from the fast, punk rock of the band's debut, *Damaged*. The years of fun and goofy anthems like "TV Party" were long gone. That sentiment may have been behind Ginn's new project, an all-instrumental hardcore power trio named Gone. In 1986, after Black Flag ceased to be a functioning band, Ginn released the first Gone album, *Let's Get Real, Real Gone for a Change*. The group would go on to release a half dozen albums over the years.

Ginn wasn't the only person taking a punk sensibility in an instrumental direction. Several bands on his label, such as Blind Idiot God and Lawndale, were pursuing the same path. By 1987, Ginn compiled enough tracks from like-minded SST groups, along with contributions from avant-garde musicians and noise artists such as Elliot Sharp and Sonic Youth's Lee Ranaldo, to release a double LP of instrumental songs. The bands on *No Age: A Compilation of SST Instrumental Music*, along with Black Flag and even early Metallica, were all creating heavy, fast, and complex instrumental music that almost dared listeners to keep up.

On the back of *No Age*, at the top of the plain white sleeve, it says WHERE THERE IS NOTHING, ANYTHING CAN HAPPEN. Ginn seems to be referring to the fact that, because none of the record's nineteen tracks have vocals or lyrics, listeners can insert their own interpretation of what the song means, or what the musicians are trying to convey through it. The time had come for people to make up their own minds about what the music meant. A dozen years later, math rock fans would have to do the same thing.

3 Rollerblade Success Story: A Short History of Math Rock

Before spending the remainder of the book talking about various aspects of math rock, I want to first present a quick overview of the genre. Please know that what follows will by no means be complete or comprehensive. In addition to thriving for more than three decades, the genre is a living, breathing art form that exists in all corners of the world. Exploring math rock's every musical avenue or sonic side street would take much more than the hundred or so pages I must work with. Instead, I'll give just enough historical grounding and musical context so that the ensuing chapters make sense. This means it's very likely I won't single out or probably even mention your favorite math rock band. It's nothing personal; I'm sure they're awesome. With that out of the way, let's begin.

Math rock website Fecking Bahamas (named after a Don Caballero song) features an interactive map called "World of Math." The map charts over 2,000 math rock bands from across the world, including 674 in America, 257 in the UK, 111 in Japan, 47 in Russia, 27 in Brazil, 24 in China, and 8 in India. Math rock is everywhere, flourishing all over the world, on a wide variety of record labels and played by people who don't share the same spoken language but who can understand each other through music. That's remarkable reach for a genre that never had a hit. But how did it happen?

In his 2022 book *Status and Culture*, W. David Marx writes about how ideas and trends develop and are ultimately adopted: "In almost all instances, new behaviors begin as an exclusive practice of smaller social groups—whether elites or outsiders—and then eventually spread to the wider population." Math rock skipped that last step. Bands never signed to major labels, got songs on mainstream radio, or appeared on the cover of glossy magazines. Rather than kill or even hurt math rock, this indifference led to its eventual survival. Being out of the limelight meant math rock could avoid the predictable rise and fall that most scenes or movements experience.

Most musical genres, after all, are a lot like people: they're born, live for a while, and then die. It's easy to imagine walking through a musical cemetery and passing huge stone mausoleums with inscriptions like BRITPOP 1993–1997. Search all you want, you won't find a tombstone for math rock. It's survived because it has no signifiers other than its sound. Grunge was associated with lots of things other than music: flannel shirts, Doc Martens, long hair. Math rock, despite being a product of the nineties, has nothing inherently "nineties" about it. Standing almost completely outside of a larger culture or style has ironically ensured that it will never go out of style.

The reason I started this book with Don Caballero is because they pretty much represent ground zero for the genre. As we'll see in the paragraphs and chapters that follow, other bands had touched upon or played some aspect of what we now consider the "math rock" sound before Don Cab did; I'm not making the claim that they invented the form or the genre. (It's also not a claim the band would ever make; they're too modest.) But in terms of being the band who first hit upon that sound and then developed it, pushed it, and saw some success with it—and were later associated almost exclusively with it,

not to mention influenced others to make similar sounds—
that honor must go to Don Caballero.

The group formed in Pittsburgh, Pennsylvania, in August
1991 as a trio with Mike Banfield on guitar, Pat Morris playing
bass, and Damon Che on drums. Ian Williams was added
later as a second guitarist. Even though they all came from
the hardcore scene, their ears were open to all kinds of stuff.
It helped that their hometown was not too big and not too
small. Pittsburgh attracted major touring acts, but not so many
that they couldn't see everything. When jazz guitarist Sonny
Sharrock played, they'd go see him. The next night they'd
queue up for minimalist composer Steve Reich. Williams also
brought to the band influences which were in short supply in
the nineties. His family had moved to the African country of
Malawi when he was nine and stayed for two years. His dad
was an academic working with the government and UNICEF
to gather health data and do research. Even though they lived
in Zomba, a modern city in the south that had once been the
capital, on the outskirts of town Williams would hear drumming
in the distance mixed with seventies Afropop. These sounds
and rhythms subliminally lodged in his consciousness and
would reappear a decade later.

The band named themselves after Guy Caballero, Joe
Flaherty's recurring character on the Canadian comedy sketch
program *SCTV*. In the show, Caballero owns the fictional SCTV
network. In one sketch, a parody of *The Godfather*, Eugene Levy
addresses Flaherty, who's assuming the role of Marlon Brando's
mafia boss, as "Don Caballero." The word "don," which in Italian
means *boss,* was often used in crime circles to denote who was
in charge; in *The Godfather*, Brando's character—the powerful
head of a crime family—is often referred to as "Don Corleone,"
despite his first name being Vito.

In the regular Guy Caballero sketches, Flaherty dresses in a white suit with a panama hat and sits in a wheelchair. Don Cab's first record, 1993's *For Respect*, pays homage to Guy Caballero beyond just the band's name. The cover features a wheelchair and, on the back, Che is dressed like the Flaherty character. In addition, seventh song on the album, "Got A Mile, Got A Mile, Got An Inch," features a long snippet from an episode of *SCTV* where someone says to Caballero, "I thought you rode a wheelchair?" and he answers, "Oh, I just use that for respect." The album was recorded by Steve Albini back when he still operated out of his house, a small bungalow where every room was taken over by the studio except the bedroom. *For Respect* was released on Touch and Go, a respected Chicago label who'd also released albums by Slint, Jesus Lizard, and Albini's two previous groups, Rapeman and Big Black.

Don Cab became the archetype for a largely instrumental genre purely by accident. They'd always meant to get a singer, but just never got around to it. They formed, practiced, wrote a bunch of songs, and started getting offered shows, all before they could find someone to front the band. Rather than let opportunities pass them by, they began playing out as an instrumental group. The format stuck and would later contribute to helping the sound travel around the world.

The group toured relentlessly behind their first LP. Two years later they followed it up with *Don Caballero 2*. There were fewer shows this time around, and the band took an extended break. The members all did their own thing. Williams had his other group, Storm and Stress, and Che had Thee Speaking Canaries. Banfield became a librarian. Nobody in the band called it a "break up," but there was a decent chance that was going to be the result. But then a funny thing happened: The seeds they'd planted with all that early touring started to pay off. An audience slowly began to grow, as did requests to play live. They reconvened for third LP, 1998's *What Burns Never Returns,* and hit the road. This time around the songs were longer and a bit more melodic; tapping, guitar loops, and a clean guitar sound that took the place of heavily distorted riffs.

The shows were well-attended, and the band was making money for the first time in its existence. Banfield came back, Che did his octopus thing, and Williams blew bubbles (a habit that started as semi-ironic shtick; if Urge Overkill could sport medallions and leisure suits, Williams would constantly chew pink gum). But the music played by Don Cab and a growing number of groups, such as Breadwinner, Tortoise, and Bastro, never grew or coalesced into a coherent scene. In the nineties—after Nirvana had sold millions of records it seemed absurdly easy for a guitar-heavy band to sign to a major label, quit their day jobs, make videos, and travel the world. Many of the groups who managed to do this came out of Chicago: Smashing Pumpkins, Liz Phair, Eleventh Dream Day, Veruca Salt, and many more. But that didn't happen for Don Cab after moving to Chicago, or for the other proto math rock bands of the day (the name "math rock" wouldn't arrive for a few more years). Sure, these groups made an important contribution to musical history, and produced a whole hell of a lot of good music, but it all never caught fire as a full-blown movement. Rather than turn into a scene or even a trend, math rock morphed into a meme. It became a self replicating idea that slyly and subtly traveled all over the world. A few decades after Don Caballero and others set the template for what we now consider to be math rock, that sound was somehow thriving in every corner of the globe.

Looking back on his contribution to the genre's founding, Don Cab's Ian Williams is humble. "I think we were good practitioners of a sound that, for a lot of people, was the first time they heard that kind of stuff. Which is cool." There was a lot in the air in Pittsburgh and then in the band's adopted home of Chicago. Williams and drummer Damon Che were taking it all in and turning those influences and sounds into something new, something that's lasted. "I still think we were channeling things we'd heard before," says Williams, "but just channeling it in new ways." Those "news ways" have since grown into a thriving global scene.

●

While Don Cab was pioneering the sound of what later became known as math rock, several other bands were also recording difficult or obtuse music that had little chance to be absorbed into the mainstream. A year after *For Respect* appeared, Louisville band Rodan released their only record, 1994's *Rusty*. The sound was off kilter, challenging, lo-fi; the emphasis was on *atmosphere* rather than *songs*. Rodan were just one of several groups who were either outright affiliated with Slint or who tried to keep that band's spirit alive by issuing expansive, and sometimes meandering, records that just as often alienated listeners as it gained them fans. This includes groups like June of 44, The For Carnation, A Minor Forest, Palace Brothers, and U.S. Maple. Each of them sometimes gets mentioned in conjunction with math rock.

Steve Albini's third band, Shellac, also released their debut record in 1994. *At Action Park* was mostly a continuation of what Albini had done with Big Black, only now he had a drummer and not just a drum machine. The music was icy, precise, heavy. While Albini's style of guitar playing had an influence on what became math rock, the bigger contribution was his work as a recording engineer (don't call him a producer). He worked on two of Don Cab's records, the first Slint LP, and numerous albums by noisy and abrasive Chicago bands. Drummer Damon Che said his drums sounded their best in Albini's capable hands. Numerous math rock groups would later work feverishly to get their drums to sound the way Che's did on the records Albini engineered.

Chavez, the group who'd had a hand in coining the term "math rock," released their first LP, *Gone Glimmering*, in 1995. The album's not remotely mathy beyond the fact that two guitars sometimes seemingly work in opposition to each other. Today, Chavez sound like any other heavy guitar outfit from the period. The fact that Chavez was called "math rock" only shows how staid and boring much of nineties music was; play one difficult chord in an open tuning and critics start running for a slide rule. Despite *Entertainment Weekly* declaring them "the future of rock" in 1996 upon the release of second LP *Ride the Fader*, Chavez never released another full-length album.

In 1999, independent label Polyvinyl released the first album by American Football, a band founded by ex-Cap'n Jazz drummer Mike Kinsella. The album created a new sound by marrying Midwest emo with twinkly math rock (there's more on emo and its relation to math rock in Chapter 4). Even though the group stopped performing or recording not long after the record came out, it's proven to be incredibly influential (Covet's Yvette Young was inspired to play in open tunings because of American Football). The band got back together in 2014 and has since released two more self-titled albums.

As the nineties ended, the math rock sound began to develop and spread. A growing number of groups, most of them based in the Midwest, were building on the momentum Don Cab had put in motion. One of those was Lynx, a Chicago-by-way-of-Boston band whose self-titled (and only) LP was released in 2000. Lynx formed in the late nineties and featured Mike Hutchins and Dave Konopka on guitar, Dale Connolly on drums, and Paul Joyce on bass. Hutchins, Konopka, and Joyce had met while attending the Massachusetts College of Art. Joyce and Hutchins were roommates in Boston's Mission Hill neighborhood; Connolly was their next-door neighbor. Prior to Lynx, Hutchins and Joyce had formed a group called Glans in which Hutchins played guitar and Joyce drummed. Glans recorded some demos in a math rock style, but never released anything. If they had, they would have been the first in a long line of math rock guitar/drum duos, paving the way for Hella, Tera Melos, Standards, and Floral. Hutchins and Joyce set Glans aside to create a bigger sound with a new band, Lynx. Recorded by Shellac bassist Bob Weston, *Lynx* was all instrumental, with dynamic and complex music; evocative and inscrutable cover art; and song titles that were either goofy ("Explosive Diarrhea") or long and nonsensical ("Look At That Table And Make It Spin In Your Head"). Math rock was quickly forming its own aesthetic. Released on tiny Chicago label Box Factory Records, *Lynx* didn't sell much, and the band broke up shortly after it came out, but it now stands as the first great math rock record of the new decade.

Over the next couple of years, more and more math rock groups—and records—began to come out of Chicago. The city, which throughout the eighties had been growing a healthy scene, absolutely erupted in the nineties. The reason so many groups flocked there was simple: it was a cheap place to live. "It was the biggest city in America that was absolutely affordable," says Jon Fine, author of *Your Band Sucks* and guitarist in Bitch Magnet and Coptic Light. "You could move there and do an art thing and get by just fine. You'd have a bunch of roommates, you got a big loft, you'd practice there.

The infrastructure was unusually good for that kind of thing." Not only could bands sustain themselves in Chicago, but an abundance of clubs and venues friendly to new bands, plus a variety of small labels willing to put out experimental or non-commercial music, meant that groups could follow any artistic impulse. Selling records, or having a career, did not have to be the goal. "Chicago is a working-class city," says Piglet drummer Matthew Parrish, "and I feel like that tends to create a specific type of unity that involves a lot of gratitude. The artists and musicians I associate with are genuinely excited about being able to share their art and there's an understanding that it's a privilege and not an entitlement, so people tend to be very respectful and welcoming here."

Guitarists Victor Villareal and Sam Zurick, who'd both been in Cap'n Jazz, formed the instrumental outfit Ghosts and Vodka along with Erik Bocek on bass and Scott Shellhamer on drums. Villareal was a brilliant and inventive musician who'd go on to play in Tim Kinsella's post-Cap'n Jazz band Joan of Arc as well as Owls, a short-lived group with Tim and Mike Kinsella (whose own project, American Football, was on hiatus at the time). Ghosts and Vodka's only record was 2001's *Precious Blood*.

Trio Dakota/Dakota released their debut, and only record, two years after Ghosts and Vodka quietly disbanded. *Shoot in the Dark* continued to push the emerging sound of math rock forward while also paying homage to the precedents set by Don Caballero and Lynx. The record contained long and humorous titles ("Just Because You Can't See My Invisible Force Field Doesn't Mean It Isn't There") along with songs that contained lots of tapping, jazz drumming, and time shifts.

Piglet were just teenagers when they released an instrumental EP named *Lava Land*. The trio consisted of Parrish on drums, Asher Weisberg on guitar, and Ezra Sandzer-Bell on bass. They took their name after the Winnie the Pooh character who'd recently gotten his own movie. Like Don Cab, Piglet toyed with the idea of having a vocalist. The band discussed getting William Zientara from Wisconsin hardcore group Managra to do some vocals, but nothing came of the idea. "We weren't a band that planned much or thought too much about what we were doing," says Parrish. "For us it was all about the thrill of the experience of challenging ourselves musically and traveling around playing." They performed at house shows and all-ages venue the Fireside Bowl but, just as with Ghosts and Vodka, Dakota/Dakota, and Lynx, they didn't stay together long. Despite never releasing a full-length album, and only existing for a few years, Piglet has been a big influence on the math rock scene and they continue to gain new fans. Just a few years after they broke up, math rock group Weye released a tribute called "We Miss You, Piglet." A decade later, Los Angeles group Escher also wrote their own appreciation, "We Also Miss You Piglet." Original copies of *Lava Land* sell for hundreds of dollars, and subsequent vinyl reissues have quickly sold out.

The catalog of math rock music was growing. Each album and EP were establishing the general aesthetics of the form and tenets of the sound. The only problem was that none of these bands were sticking around. The sound was in danger of getting stuck in the bubble of Chicago. The unintended side effect of living in a city where you could get by playing in an experimental rock band was that groups had no drive to do anything else. They'd form a band, play some shows, put out a cassette, and then quickly move on to something else. If math rock was going to amount to something other than a detour or an asterisk, or exist outside of just a regional setting, it was going to need a band that was going to last. Even forefathers of the scene, Don Caballero, sat out most of the 2000s. After Don

Cab's fourth record, 2000's *American Don*, the members once again went their separate ways. Guitarist Ian Williams moved to New York, where he hooked up with ex-Lynx member Dave Konopka. Along with ex-Helmet drummer John Stanier and musician Tyondai Braxton (son of jazz saxophonist Anthony Braxton), they formed Battles, signing to UK electronic label Warp. Battles was new and exciting, but it was not math rock. (Konopka would go on to use his graphic design degree to create Battles record sleeves and posters until he left the band in 2018.) Don Cab drummer Damon Che returned to an earlier project, recording an album as The Speaking Canaries in 2003. He finally reconvened Don Cab with a new lineup later in the decade, but it proved short-lived, producing just one LP before disbanding.

In 2005, a band put out an album that was not only a milestone in the history of math rock, but it proved to be the introduction to a group that was going to develop and push the genre over several subsequent releases. The fact that the band came from Japan showed that the sound and influence of math rock had indeed been able to escape the confines of the Windy City. It was just the beginning of a musical diaspora that continues to this day.

•

Tokyo-based Toe, whose name is often stylized as toe or T.O.E. (which stands for either *theory of everything* or *testamentary occasional eudaemonism*), consists of Yamazaki Hirokazu and Mino Takaaki on guitar, Yamane Satoshi on bass, and Kashikura Takashi on drums. The musical backgrounds of the members show how related genres fed into the math rock sound. Prior to Toe, Hirokazu and Yamane had been in a screamo band called Dove, Mino was in the emo outfit Pop Catcher, and Kashikura played in the hardcore group Reach. In 2000, the four started to play together as Toe. An early inspiration was Ghosts and Vodka, Hirokazu telling *The Japan Times* in 2010, "I loved their emotional guitar music without vocals."

The band began with Hirokazu and Takaaki working on songs together. Satoshi was next to join. Filling out the lineup was Takaaki's friend Takashi on drums. The band started playing shows and put out a few singles before the release of their debut album. While subsequent records and song titles abandoned the math rock convention of being long or crazy (or both), the name of that first LP was math rock perfection: *The Book About My Idle Plot on a Vague Anxiety*. The cover, a close-up photo of a baby deer's head tilted ninety degrees clockwise, was also impeccably enigmatic. The record was released on small, independent labels in Japan (Catune) and America (Topshelf).

While it's not as heavy as any of the Chicago bands, *The Book About My Idle Plot* has a lightness and intricacy that was beyond the reach (or desire) of first wave groups. But whereas some later math rock albums would push that same lightness into the realm of twinkly meandering, Toe's debut never becomes mere background music. The songs are always engaging, lively, and interesting.

That being said, the LP instantly throws you a curveball: Opening track "反逆する風景" ("Rebellious Landscape") starts with an offkilter loop of standup bass set against weird pulses, snapping, and electric piano—setting the stage for an experimental rock record, something like Joan of Arc or Storm and Stress. This might explain the song's title; for a band with two guitarists and a star drummer, creating this kind of musical landscape (with no guitar or drumming) is indeed rebellious. Further confusing things, the next thing you hear is a voice rapping in Japanese. The voice belongs to Takeshi Osumi (also known as Big-O), from the Japanese rap act Shakkazombie. After less than a minute, "Rebellious Landscape" is over, and the album begins in earnest.

The second track, "孤独の発明" ("Invention of Loneliness"), is not only Toe's most popular song, but it's also probably the most perfect embodiment of the band's sound (and genius). There are numerous pauses, abundant glimmery guitar, and Takashi's drumming is off the charts. What's amazing about the track is how much space is in it. For a band filled with four adept musicians, everyone's underplaying; even the drums occasionally hold back to give the tune air to breathe. At a bit more than two minutes in (the song is relatively brief by math rock standards; it's under three-and-a-half minutes, the perfect pop song length), a scream is buried in the mix. This only adds to the tune's overall ennui. Was that a desperate howl for help, a cathartic cry of relief, or merely a musician's frustration at having blown a take (akin to Ringo's "I've got blisters on my fingers!" at the end of "Helter Skelter")? Sometimes, when I listen to the song, I'm not even sure the shriek is coming from a human.

Throughout the album, Hirokazu and Takaaki's guitar lines are precise and economical, favoring single notes over chords. They also pretty much completely avoid the standard math rock techniques of finger picking or tapping. The real star of the show is Takashi on drums. For all of Steve Albini's vaunted ability to record drums, Takashi shows that there's a lot more to the instrument than just sounding HUGE. He plays with a fluidity and grace unmatched in rock circles; his playing is on the level of the world's best jazz drummers. Takashi started playing drums as soon as he could. Growing up in Kawasaki, a large city located between Tokyo and Yokohama, his sister was a member of the school choir. When Takashi entered first grade, he was able to join as well, playing percussion. (Choirs are a big deal in Japan. Almost all public and private schools have them, and there are choir competitions each year.) Some older junior high kids showed him the ropes, starting with quarter notes and eighth notes. By the time he made it to junior high himself, kids were forming their own groups (in addition to being into skateboarding and rollerblading). Takashi played in several cover bands in different genres (punk, acid jazz, rock) before joining hardcore band Reach. Hearing Takashi drum on Reach's first album, 1999's *A Disc Full of Signs*, you can hear the wiry and frenetic intensity he'd soon bring to Toe.

Toe, as a band, arrived fully formed and *The Book About My Idle Plot* is a milestone of the genre. Over time they'd expand on the math rock sound, adding touches like acoustic guitar, Rhodes piano, and vocals. And while Toe didn't go on to be hugely prolific (they've only released two other albums), their debut alone has earned them a place in math rock history.

The year *The Book About My Idle Plot* came out, another Japanese band, Lite, released their first record. Like Toe, Lite is from Tokyo, has four members, and plays a mostly instrumental form of math rock. They refuse to let that last point define them. "We don't have vocals," guitarist Nobuyuki Takeda told *Vice* in 2013, "but we don't think of ourselves as a band without vocals. The guitar phrases pick up some of that slack, and the drums stand out in certain places, things like that. The things I have to say do not require a singer." The group has released six albums and has toured internationally numerous times. Toe and Lite are just two of dozens of Japanese math rock bands that have formed and released records since *The Book About My Idle Plot* appeared in 2005.

In addition to all the activity in Japan, over the ensuing decades more and more countries produced math rock bands.

In the UK you had This Town Needs Guns (later shortened to TTNG), Clever Girl, Three Trapped Tigers, Alpha Male Tea Party, Cleft, Delta Sleep, and more. In France there was Totorro and Touccan. Tom's Story came out of the Philippines, Rosa Parks hailed from Hungary, Elephant Gym emerged from Taiwan, and Foco formed in Ecuador. In the United States, the sound eventually spread to well beyond just Chicago. CHON, Tera Melos, Covet, Giraffes? Giraffes!, Floral, and Standards all came out of the West Coast. Back East there was Science Penguin, Invalids, Turing Machine, Shake The Baby Until The Love Comes Out, and Cuzco.

Several independent labels cropped up to release music by these newly minted math rock groups. Topshelf, the small Portland label who signed Toe, also put out albums by domestic and international artists, including Lite, Giraffes? Giraffes!, Rooftops, and Standards. Sargent House, a Los Angeles label launched around the same time as Topshelf, has released records by Hella, Tera Melos, Maps & Atlases, and Adebisi Shank. New Jersey's Choke Artist, formed in 2012, boasts the excellent groups Invalids and Floral (in addition to sporting the admirable motto CREATE CULTURE). And while none of these labels ever intended to be devoted exclusively to math rock, by signing and promoting prominent or little-known math rock bands, they've done a lot to advance the genre. Getting signed to a label meant not just getting physical goods into the hands of fans, but it helped ensure tour support, enabling groups to travel beyond their local scenes and hometowns. These labels have flourished; what began as shoestring operations, operated out of dorm rooms and garages, would prove so successful they would sign huge rosters of bands from around the world and hire full-time employees.

The last element needed to ensure the survival and spread of math rock was the internet. The arrival of the World Wide

Web in the late nineties meant that previously inaccessible subcultures were suddenly exposed and accessible by anyone, anywhere, at any time; the underground was now just a few keyboard clicks away. "Without the internet, no one would have really heard of us," TTNG's bass player Henry Tremain told *God is in the TV* in 2013. "Well, there are always these really interesting small scenes where really obscure bands from different places get known, but only in small cliques. But with the internet, it's kind of expanded those cliques." What might have taken a group like Lynx or Piglet months to achieve on a local level, and only by arduously playing old bowling alleys or parties, could now be achieved on a global scale almost overnight. (More on this in Chapter 7.) The introduction of Myspace in 2003 also meant that new fans could not only just learn about math rock or hear some songs, but bands could reach out directly to fans. This led to things like playthrough videos, selling tabs, and entire websites devoted to the genre.

Thirty years after Don Caballero and the other Chicago groups created a new sound and aesthetic, math rock was everywhere.

4   Oh Messy Life: Genres Related to Math Rock

Like any other musical genre, the boundaries of "math rock" are porous and often subjectively defined (what I consider to be math rock may differ from what you think is math rock). The slipperiness of the style also means there's considerable overlap with other genres, namely, post-rock, mathcore, and emo.

Post-rock was put in motion by many of the same impulses that birthed math rock. A new generation of musicians was tired of adhering to the same old song structures; they wanted to wrench a new kind of sound from the basic rock band configuration of guitar, bass, and drums. As Bitch Magnet guitarist Jon Fine wrote in his 2015 autobiography *Your Band Sucks*, "there were so many things you could do with rock music, once you started ignoring all the rules." Groups like Mogwai, Godspeed You! Black Emperor, Sigur Rós, and Explosions in the Sky did exactly that, creating a new kind of rock music that favored texture over traditional song structures and traded choruses for crescendos. (Fine also followed his own advice; after Bitch Magnet broke up, he went on to found the band Vineland as well as the post-rock supergroup Coptic Light.)

Before coining the term "post-rock" in 1994, critic Simon Reynolds formulated his ideas in a *Melody Maker* article from the previous summer titled "American Alternative Rock: A Survey of the State of the Art." Noting how bands like Seefeel,

Insides, and Stereolab were incorporating elements of techno, ambient, and dub into their music, Reynolds wrote that these groups "probably don't even warrant the term 'rock' anymore, since they're based around layers and textures, rather than riff-dynamics, around using the studio-as-instrument rather than simulating a 'live' band."

Like math rock, much of post-rock is instrumental and songs often stretch well past the five—or six—(or even ten)-minute mark. Due to these characteristics, post-rock isn't considered terribly commercial, and most post-rock bands are on small, independent labels. However, in the post-Nirvana gold rush of the nineties—despite the music's unconventional sound and limited commercial appeal—post-rock bands were courted by major labels. At least for a while.

Paul Heck was a New York-based A&R executive at Warner Bros. in the late nineties. As one of the biggest labels in the world, Warner Bros. had spent much of the previous years hoovering up the best alternative bands, including R.E.M., Flaming Lips, Dinosaur Jr., Built To Spill, and many more. Heck, a lifelong and rabid music fan, was fresh from working with a number of alternative and indie rock acts while putting together AIDS charity records for the Red Hot organization. At Warner Bros. Heck wanted to look beyond the current scene and try to sign some of the next wave of great bands. He loved groups like Tortoise, Moonshake, Laika, Stereolab, and Broadcast, even if no one could agree on what to call them. "It was shorthand," he says of the term "post-rock," "a way to reference a loose grouping of bands, all of whom would probably disavow the label. Like a lot of music genre shorthand, it now references an era as much, if not more so, than the bands who were considered a part of it. In the mid-nineties it was an exciting area of music. In fact, it still is."

At his first big meeting in Los Angeles to discuss the label's roster, one of the West Coast A&R executives said to him, "You're the post-rock guy." Heck was both bemused and surprised. "That was news to me, but I didn't mind the association. Post-rock was a new thing, and if the perception was I was the guy with my finger on the post-rock pulse, that was cool." (While in California, Heck met Squirrel Bait and Slint guitarist and vocalist Brian McMahan, who was working as an A&R assistant. Heck recalls, "He seemed nice.")

Heck's time at Warner Bros. ended without him signing any group and, for the most part, post-rock bands stayed on small, independent labels. In the UK, that didn't stop groups from making a splash. John Peel was a huge fan of the Scottish group Mogwai, inviting the band to record numerous sessions and playing them often on his BBC radio show. In 2003, the last year Peel presided over the Festive Fifty (he died the following year), the annual list of the year's best songs, Mogwai had two tracks in the top ten ("Hunted by a Freak" at number three and "Ratts of the Capital" at number six). Post-rock bands also appeared on the cover of influential music papers like the *New Musical Express*. It may have been an independent scene, but it was hardly underground; Mogwai even scored a number one album in the UK in 2021 with their tenth studio LP, *As the Love Continues*.

One of the biggest ingredients in post-rock is the use of dynamics: tracks that follow a pattern of quiet-loud-quiet. Boston band the Pixies had been doing this since the eighties, and Nirvana's huge 1991 hit "Smells Like Teen Spirit" is probably the best and most well-known example. Post-rock bands took this idea to extremes, writing and performing songs that began *very* quiet and became *very* loud. This went well beyond just stepping on a distortion pedal. Post-rock songs often featured huge and furious crescendos that crashed like thunder, placed between passages of pastoral and nearly inaudible music (a user on Reddit described these tracks as going from "I can't hear what they're playing" to "I can't hear anything").

Mogwai's "Like Herod," from the band's 1997 debut, is a perfect example of the quiet-loud-quiet dynamic found in post-rock. It's a long track, with several instrumental peaks and valleys. After three minutes of soft and spidery music that sounds an awful lot like Slint (it's easy to tell why the band initially called the track "Slint"), the guitars become heavy and distorted, the drumming more frenzied. After nearly two minutes of noise, it retreats to the quiet passage from earlier. The pattern repeats before the song finally ends in a drone of feedback. When played live, "Like Herod" often stretches to well beyond the nearly twelve minutes that appeared on *Mogwai Young Team*. A version recorded for the BBC clocked in at 18:30.

Another great example of post-rock's penchant for dynamics is "Svefn-g-englar," the first track off Icelandic band Sigur Rós's second album, 1999's *Ágætis byrjun*. For most of the tune's ten-minute running time, the song is slow and beautiful, accompanied by a haunting and echoey ping that sounds something like a sonar signal. But after about six minutes, the tune bursts into a short passage of raucous drumming and heavy guitar. Unlike the Mogwai track, the clamorous interlude lasts less than a minute, and then it's back to the track's ethereal beauty.

None of this was entirely new. Rock bands had been pummeling audiences with volume ever since rock music was invented. For years, The Who held the record for being the loudest band in the world, once playing a concert in London that could have drowned out a jet engine. In the nineties,

English group My Bloody Valentine pushed the limits of volume and feedback in their live shows. Performing their 1998 track "You Made Me Realise," the group settles into an extended instrumental passage that's become known as the "holocaust section." The song, which is well under four minutes on record, often extends anywhere from ten to twenty minutes, most of that being ear-splitting feedback. The band itself acknowledges the discomfort; at concerts, earplugs are handed out as you walk in.

Post-rock's over reliance on dynamics can make the genre slightly formulaic. Whenever I listen to bands that employ this technique, I'm always waiting for the big moment when everything's going to get LOUD. And then, when the musicians are going apeshit, all I can do is wonder how long it's going to last before resolving back to the pretty music heard at the beginning. For bands like Sigur Rós, those apeshit moments don't tend to last long; for other groups, like Godspeed You! Black Emperor and Mogwai, they seem to be the point.

Another limiting aspect is post-rock's generally restricted sonic palette. A lot of songs are built around the repetition of fairly standard chords and notes. Sometimes this can create a great deal of drama, like in King Crimson's proto post-rock track "Starless," where the longer Robert Fripp plays the same note, the more tension is ratcheted up. At other times, it can feel like a slog to sit through a ten-minute track that only features two or three chords. (That extended loud part of "You Made Me Realise" mentioned earlier is the band whacking away on one chord for all that time.) Post-rock also often features fairly straightforward time signatures, and the structure of the tracks—besides rising and falling—follow more or less the same tempo; songs get heavier and louder, but seldom much faster or slower. Post-rock is all about rise and fall, as opposed to the sideways meandering and maze-like journey of math rock.

Post-rock and math rock also wildly diverge in their general attitude and presentation. Canadian group Godspeed You! Black Emperor are a shadowy anti-capitalist collective who avoid social media and interviews and have only released two official band photos in their 25+ years of existence. They consider their work to be "protest music." Contrast this with math rock bands such as Pajama Day (two adults who perform in pajamas) or Standards (the cover of their 2022 album *Fruit Island* looks like a package of gummy bears). Post-rock is deadly serious. Math rock, not so much.

●

Like post-rock, mathcore formed in the nineties alongside math rock, and it's still around today. Both mathcore and math rock share many of the same characteristics: tempo changes, odd time signatures, dexterous and complicated guitar parts, virtuoso drumming, and complex song structures. And while plenty of math rock bands, in the early years, employed distorted guitars and had a metal edge to their sound (Don Caballero's first album, *For Respect*, could be considered a heavy metal record), mathcore bands take a metal sound to the extreme. The genre quickly became a combination of math rock and thrash or speed metal: punishing, pummeling music that's played super-fast and ultra-loud. When songs have vocals (which is often; the most prominent mathcore bands, such as Dillinger Escape Plan, have singers), the words are screamed, shouted, or delivered in a guttural growl that's not too far removed from the "Cookie Monster" vocals of grindcore and metalcore.

Another thing mathcore and math rock bands have in common is an aversion to the name. In an article from 2020 on the hard rock/heavy metal website *The Pit*, the editors sympathized with all those mathcore groups who hate the term. "I get it, who wants their music to be compared to their least favorite high school class?"

Mathcore was pioneered by bands such as Botch, Converge, and Rorschach, all of which spent years crisscrossing the country playing sweaty basement shows to pissed-off teenagers. Many were signed to independent record labels, such as Victory, and had spent years in the vegan straight edge hardcore scene. Mathcore was their way of pushing their already extreme sound even further away from the mainstream. Less political than post-rock, and not as brainy as math rock, mathcore bands tend to be just plain angry. Most mathcore iconography, like death metal, focuses on horror film imagery; band logos tend to look like a jumble of twigs. A few heavy and experimental math rock groups, such as Hella and Tera Melos, cross over into mathcore territory but, for the most part, you won't find much overlap (not many fans of Covet also like Coalesce).

While the more popular mathcore bands, the ones with singers who just sound like sped up metal, or heavier emo, aren't doing much to push the form forward, a few groups at the margins of the scene are doing interesting things. One of those bands is Behold … The Arctopus. (Even though they largely dropped the ellipsis in 2012, I can't resist using it at least once because it makes their name sound so … dramatic.) Behold The Arctopus was founded as a duo in 2001 by guitarists Colin Marston and Mike Lerner. They met at NYU; Marston was studying music technology, while Lerner was working toward a degree in jazz composition. Since releasing their debut album in 2007, Lerner and Marston have gone through a succession of drummers. However, they've never let this stop them (not even at the beginning; rather than wait until they had a drummer, their first demo featured a drum machine and was released as *We Need a Drummer*). The band's records usually sport cryptic or unintelligible titles, such as *Nano Nucleonic Cyborg Summoning*, though some individual songs retain the charm and goofy wit of math rock ("You Will Be Reincarnated As An Imperial Attack Space Turtle").

Two ingredients are key to the band's unique and highly engaging sound. While Lerner plays more or less a standard guitar (it features seven strings as opposed to the usual six), Marston plays a Warr guitar. An instrument closely related to a Chapman stick (which is played by King Crimson and Peter Gabriel bassist Tony Levin), the Warr guitar was invented by Mark Warr in 1991. It features an incredibly wide neck and can be configured with anywhere from eight to fourteen strings. Known as a "touch guitar," it's played almost exclusively by tapping (we'll hear more about this in Chapter 6). Marston plays a 12-string model, with a set of bass strings for his left hand and guitar strings for his right. This allows him to essentially play basslines and leads at the same time, turning the instrument into a kind of guitar piano. All of Marston's tapping on the Warr guitar lends Behold The Arctopus a jazzy and proggy sound not heard in many of their mathcore contemporaries. "The Warr guitar and 7-string guitar make for a great combo," Lerner told *RVA Magazine* in 2013. "There's no set rules and we'll go from parts where it sounds like two guitars and a bass to parts where it sounds like two lead guitars, to three-part counterpoint lines. Having this wide palette of sounds allows us to reach further in whatever direction we choose."

The other aspect that makes much of Behold The Arctopus's music special is the fact that, for years, the band composed their songs on a computer as traditionally notated music. Once a piece of was written, they would then learn how to play it on their instruments. This process began when they didn't have a drummer, and Marston would have to painstakingly program drum parts. He found that writing in musical notation form, rather than on a guitar, made him freer with his parts and less likely to revert to standard riffs or musical clichés. (Broadway composer and lyricist Stephen Sondheim would often write away from the piano for the same reason.) This resulted in compositions that were startlingly original, but also hard to play.

The band knows that their songs can be difficult to listen. That's why they opt to make LPs that don't last very long. "With music that's of this sort of density," Marston told *Mathcore Index* in 2019, "I think it's nice to have a short album. It's a little more digestible for people." He's right. Behold The Arctopus create amazingly original music, but listening to it can quickly turn into a test of endurance. Jagged, frantic, and intensely fractured, they make Jesus Lizard sound like The Monkees. Writing about the band's most recent record, 2020's *Hapeleptic Overtrove*, Phil Freeman noted, "Nothing else sounds like this, and very little likely ever will. Most people don't want to think this hard about music, including musicians."

Another interesting band with a foot in the worlds of both mathcore and math rock is Orthrelm. The duo of drummer Josh Blair and guitarist Mick Barr has put out a number of records since forming in 2000 (including, in 2006, a split single with Behold The Arctopus). Despite being just two guys playing two instruments, Orthrelm's music is mind-bogglingly complex (in addition to being super heavy). Their early work featured practically no repetition of chords or notes, giving their songs—which range anywhere from twenty-two seconds to forty-five minutes long—a disorienting, maze-like feel. The pieces feel improvised if not totally random, even though they're compositions. Finn Mckenty, on his YouTube channel Punk Rock MBA, describes Orthrelm as "the hardcore version of Ornette Coleman," adding that their music is almost "a meta comment on their own genre." Orthrelm not only shares Behold The Arctopus penchant for inscrutable record names (e.g., *Norildivoth Crallos-Lomrixth Urthiln*), they go farther by also giving individual songs crazy titles that are both unpronounceable and just plain odd: "Aonkrit Iom-Spear," "Hixor Sparrill Monce," "Scelxenak." These are all words that, like the band's name itself, have been made up by Mick Barr. Despite its complexity and abrasiveness, much of Orthrelm's work, the same as Behold The Arctopus, would sit nicely alongside the harder edges of math rock. Barr even made an improvised record in 2006 with Hella's Zach Hill called *Shred Earthship*. Like math rock, if you dig under the surface of mathcore, there are lots of interesting things to discover.

•

Even though mathcore features the word "math" in its name, the genre that shares the most DNA with math rock (and the most fans) is emo. In a lot of people's minds, the two are synonymous. Plenty of groups label themselves as such, and numerous guitar tutorials on YouTube categorize their lessons as teaching "math rock/emo," as if the styles were two sides of the same coin.

In the early eighties, Washington, DC, was a hotbed of punk activity. For years, the town had seen a bevy of hardcore bands forming and playing shows around town: Minor Threat, Bad Brains, The Teen Idles, S.O.A. (Henry Rollins's first group), Youth Brigade, Scream (which featured a teenage Dave Grohl on drums), and a dozen others. As the scene grew larger, it began to attract vandals and thugs, meatheads drawn merely to the violence of the scene. Several of the more thoughtful hardcore groups—led by Guy Picciotto's Rites of Spring—wanted to take things in a new direction. In the summer of 1985, Rites of Spring kicked off what came to be known as Revolution Summer. Picciotto's band, along with a few like-minded groups, staged political protests against Apartheid at the South African embassy and tried to turn the tide against what it saw as increasingly violent and macho behavior at hardcore shows.

In January 1986, this new scene and style of music was given a name: emo-core. Skateboard magazine *Thrasher*, in its column *Notes from the Underground*, coined the term.

> There's a new form of performance occurring out in Washington, D.C. It goes by the name of Emo-Core or Emotional Core. Bands like Embrace (featuring Ian McKaye [sic]), Rites of Spring, Beefeater, among others, are taking the severe Intensity of an emotional projection and adding it totally into their respective live sets. Crowds are said to be left in tears from the intensity.

Bands took an instant disliking to the name. Not long after the magazine came out, MacKaye (perhaps also miffed that *Thrasher* misspelled his name) railed against the term while onstage with his post-Minor Threat band Embrace at D.C's 9:30 Club: "I must say, 'emo-core' must be the stupidest fucking thing I've ever heard in my entire life." The argument that MacKaye and others would make over the years was that the name and idea were ridiculous because hardcore had *always* been emotional. While the point is valid on the surface, what MacKaye and others fail to realize is that the word *emotional* is a singular signifier for a whole rainbow of emotions. Anger, confusion, disappointment, and disillusionment are indeed all emotions that hardcore had been dealing with in abundance for years. *Thrasher* was pointing out that the hardcore scene was witnessing the unveiling of a host of *new* emotions which had heretofore been seen as verboten: vulnerability, self-doubt, sensitivity. And whereas Rites of Spring, from a sonic angle, resembled other hardcore bands at the time, MacKaye's Embrace were indeed dealing with these subjects in a manner that was more tuneful and honest than their peers. In the song "Building," MacKaye sings about being a failure, things not working out the way that he'd planned, and not being able to express how he feels; the track wouldn't be out of place on a Smiths record. During "Give Me Back" MacKaye pleads with unseen forces to "give me back my feelings" (while also declaring, "My emotions are my enemies").

This was indeed sensitive, raw, and emotional stuff, especially when compared to the other hardcore records released that year. Corrosion of Conformity's debut album, *Animosity,* was the typical blast of misanthropic thrash. *Frankenchrist*, by The Dead Kennedys, was loopy satire. Black Flag, who released three records that year (including their instrumental EP), were dealing in their usual subjects of murder, death, and mayhem. *Thrasher*'s term for Embrace and Rites of Spring made quite a lot of sense, whether the bands thought so or not.

After forming in 1984, Rites of Spring released one self-titled album the following year and split by 1986. They didn't even tour much or play more than a handful of shows. Embrace followed suit, breaking up not long after the show where MacKaye decried emo. They left behind one influential record. Picciotto and Rites of Spring drummer Brendan Canty would form Fugazi along with MacKaye and bassist Joe Lally in 1987. (For the record, Picciotto also hated the term "emo.")

As the eighties turned into the nineties, and more bands began to be termed emo, the name took on a new and disturbing life as an epithet. In an essay for *Talkhouse*, Norman Brannon from Texas in the Reason wrote about how the term had transformed from descriptive to derisive. "In New York City, being called 'emo' was akin to being called 'soft,' and that alone was the kind of thing that got you beat down on the Bowery right before somebody stole your Doc Martens." Matt Mullen, in a 2017 *Interview* article entitled "The secret history of emo music" agreed with Brannon's assessment, writing "the term was hurled as an insult at hardcore bands." This goes a long way toward explaining why many bands fought so hard not to be associated with the genre.

The math rock/emo connection began in the early nineties thanks almost entirely to a young group from the Chicago suburbs called Cap'n Jazz. The band was formed by brothers Tim and Mike Kinsella (Mike drummed, Tim sang), along with guitarist Victor Villarreal and bassist Sam Zurick. All four were teenagers. Mike Kinsella, who joined the group when he was twelve, was still a teenager when the group split up in 1995. Unlike other bands in their local hardcore scene, Cap'n Jazz played music that was ferocious but also intricate. In addition to Tim Kinsella's blood curdling scream (give a listen to "Oh Messy Life"), there was a dimension and depth to the music that went far beyond the usual punk energy. This was thanks to Villarreal. Classically trained, he added a huge amount of musicality to what otherwise would have been just another garage band of angry suburban white kids. Cap'n Jazz's unique and tuneful take on hardcore resulted in them being tagged "emo."

As the nineties wore on, and labels like Jade Tree and Revelation signed up more and more second-wave emo bands, the term grew wide enough to encompass groups like Sunny Day Real Estate and Bright Eyes, bands who had only a passing resemblance to what had come before. The pop-punk of The Get Up Kids and Jimmy Eat World also got tagged as emo. As the decade welcomed the new millennium, an even newer wave of emo bands began to have real hits and cross over completely to the mainstream. Fall Out Boy, My Chemical Romance, and Paramore sold millions of albums, filled huge stadiums, and were all over what was left of MTV. The internet, which had appeared in the previous decade but hadn't become ubiquitous until the oughties, helped propel these bands to stardom. Through websites like LiveJournal and Myspace, fans learned about new music, connected with each other and, in some cases, connected with the bands. Emo—now linked with signifiers such as dyed black hair, skinny jeans, and eyeliner—was everywhere.

While the more conventional emo bands were selling all those compact discs, the groups formed out of the ashes of Cap'n Jazz, most notably Tim Kinsella's Joan of Arc, Mike Kinsella's American Football, and Sam Zurick and Victor Villareal's Ghosts and Vodka, would each find favor with math rock fans. Joan of Arc was the most experimental of the three. The group lasted from 1995 to 2020 and released over a dozen albums of shapeshifting and mostly respected indie rock (give *The Gap* a listen; it's not as bad as you've heard).

Mike Kinsella's American Football has proven to be the most successful of the post Cap'n Jazz bands. The group's 1999 self-titled debut is now recognized as a musical milestone, and Kinsella's complex guitar style and crystal-clear tone has become known as "twinkly emo math rock." Pretty much every "emo/math rock" tutorial on YouTube basically teaches the American Football sound. (The site is also home to dozens of covers of "Never Meant," the group's most popular song.) American Football also features jazzy drumming as opposed to straight ahead beats, not to mention non-math rock elements like vocals and trumpet.

American Football's success and eventual ubiquity wasn't something anyone saw coming. After Polyvinyl quietly released the record, and the band played a few shows, American Football broke up. The record, through word of mouth and a growing reputation spurred by the internet, grew in popularity and stature over time. Indeed, it became a sort of mini-*Spiderland*, inspiring new generations of fans and musicians who never had a chance to see the band live.

The house pictured on the cover, located not far from the campus of the University of Illinois at Urbana-Champaign, has even become a destination for emo fans to pose for selfies. In fact, when the group and its record label heard in 2022 that the house was going to be torn down to make way for condominiums, they joined together to buy it. American Football reunited in 2014 for a series of concerts and have also released new music, issuing two more self-titled records (in 2016 and 2019). Both LPs have added to rather than diminish the group's legacy. (Not to be outdone, a band in Wuhan, China, has winningly named themselves Chinese Football.)

While math rock purists might reject the group for being too lightweight (or simply dismiss them due to their association with emo), American Football's application of straightforward lyrics sung over complex music makes them the perfect entry point for any friend or family member interested in exploring the genre.

5 Savage Composition: Writing Math Rock

Pink Floyd's seminal 1973 album *Dark Side of the Moon* begins and ends with a heartbeat. That rhythm—steady, even, pulsating—forms the backbone of the entire record, just as our own heartbeats begin and end our lives. When we hear something with that steady of a beat, we can't help but lock onto it, lulled by its comforting and circular nature. Most popular music seeks to replicate this, offering a rhythm you can clap along with or nod your head to (think of tracks like "Stayin' Alive" by the Bee Gees or Blondie's "Heart of Glass"). The pulse in those hits is so steady and primal it's almost impossible to not move *some* part of your body when you hear them. Even young children will find it easy to keep time to the beat. "Rhythm turns listeners into participants," writes Oliver Sacks in his 2007 book *Musicophilia*. "It is very difficult to remain detached, to resist being drawn into the rhythm of chanting or dancing." But what happens when you encounter something a bit unsteady, a rhythm out of sorts? What happens when your heart skips a beat or two, or three?

Tempo shifts and odd time signatures have been a part of music for centuries. Classical composers would often employ these time signatures, or change the tempo of a piece, to create contrast or add expression. Let me pause for a quick definition: A time signature consists of two parts: how many beats are in a measure and what the note values of those beats are. For example, in the straightforward world of 4/4—or common time—you'll be getting four quarter notes in each measure, so each time you tap your foot to the beat, you're tapping a single quarter note. When a time signature is referred to as "odd," it doesn't mean it's strange or out of the ordinary, though it may in fact sound as such. Instead, an odd time signature—also known as a complex, irregular, unusual, or asymmetric time signature—is one where there are unequal beats in a measure, meaning instead of two or four beats there are three, five, seven, nine, or eleven. Modern-day songwriters, like Palm's Eve Alpert, utilize odd time signatures for the same reasons that composers did hundreds of years ago. "In Palm, rhythms are often used to express anxiety or feeling unsettled," Alpert told *She Shreds* in 2017, "like there's no ground beneath your feet."

Feet have been a crucial part of pop music for decades. Musicians use them to keep time, and audiences do much the same, tapping their toes to a song's beat. To do that, however, the music must unfold in a certain and likely way. "Rhythm is a game of expectation," writes Daniel J. Levitan in his 2006 book *This Is Your Brain on Music*. "When we tap our feet we are predicting what is going to happen in the music next." What math rock does is scramble and deny the calculations your brain makes as it listens to the music. You can try and tap a foot, or clap along, but it's difficult when the beat skips, changes, or disappears, slowing down and then speeding up. The feeling is akin to trying to stroll steadily on a moving walkway that's jerking frontwards and backwards; you can't lock onto any kind of rhythm or stride because the floor keeps moving. Your feet don't know where to land.

A lot of modern and mainstream bands have employed odd time signatures in their songs. "The Crunge," by Led Zeppelin, is in 9/8 and Rush's "Limelight," is in 7/4 while Radiohead's "15

Steps," is in 5/4 and another of their tracks, "2+2=5," is in 7/8. In a song that's in 5/4 or 7/8—because odd numbers can't be divided in half—that extra beat is what makes it hard to clap along. To a listener not accustomed to hearing songs in irregular meters, it may sound like the track is stuttering or skipping (that steady heartbeat opening *Dark Side of the Moon* suddenly has arrhythmia). Our brains must work harder to latch onto, and keep hold of, the beat.

Of course, types of rhythm, and what's considered an irregular time signature, show our Western bias. Many countries' popular songs are rooted in meters that would seem strange to most ears. "In countries such as Bulgaria, Greece, Macedonia, Serbia, Turkey and somewhat in Hungary, Romania and others," Yugoslavian pianist and composer Koshanin wrote on his blog in 2018, "meters such as 7/8, 9/8, 11/8 and 13/8 in all their variations are so prominently featured in traditional folk music that they are truly an inseparable element—a staple feature, often to an extent that the music written in an even meter becomes an exception to the rule."

When a tricky time signature works, it's because the song calls for or demands it; you just can't imagine hearing it any other way. Talking about the complex compositions of Slint, a band whose influence hangs heavy over math rock, Bitch Magnet guitarist Jon Fine told me, "You couldn't do what they did and play in 4/4." The risk is when bands write in odd time signatures for no real reason. "If you're just jumping from time signature to time signature for the sake of it," says Palm's Eve Alpert, "you'll probably end up with something cold, calculated, and uncompelling on a human level."

For singer and guitarist Tim Kinsella, a song's time signature should exist solely in the background, not something that announces itself to the audience. "The music is about creating a feeling and if you're good at it," he told *Aquarium Drunkard* in 2022, "it's about creating layered feelings that create a different resonate feeling." Kinsella also hates being lumped into the math rock scene because "we've never counted a song in our lives." He's not alone. Most musicians are unaware of the time signatures their songs are in, at least initially.

"We don't think about time signatures at all!" declares Luke Palascak, singer and guitarist in Pretend. The band's drummer, Joel Morgan, agrees. "I actually don't think any of us know time signatures outside of 4/4," says Morgan. "When people ask me about signatures, I have no idea what they are saying. Then they explain to me what timings we were playing in, and my response is 'cool!'" Instead of coming up with flashy or difficult-on-purpose time signatures, Pretend prefers to place a strong emphasis on feeling, intuition, and mood, playing off of and exploring the atmosphere (and sounds) that emerge from the members playing together. If that means they avoid writing in common time or end up with a song that's eight or ten minutes long, that's just the way it is. And if those results are something you're not likely to hear on the radio, the band doesn't care about that, either. "Time, as it pertains to seconds or minutes," says bassist Mike Russell, "part length, song length, or time signatures is never discussed within the band. Nor is commerciality."

Having a song in an odd time signature doesn't automatically make it inaccessible to an average listener or mean that people at home, or at a concert, won't be able to enjoy it. "People can subdivide better than you think they can," says Rooftops guitarist Drew Fitchette, "and people can bob their head to something even if the time signature is changing, as long as the tempo stays relatively consistent. When you lose people is when things slow down or speed up."

Fitchette knows this from experience. Once, on tour with Rooftops, the band played a show in La Crosse, Wisconsin, at a bar filled with Army reservists. The band didn't know what to expect but feared the worst. "These guys are going to kick the fucking shit out of us," Drew remembers thinking. Rooftops nervously took the stage and played their usual set of math rock. Afterwards, people came up to the players, telling them, "I've never heard music like that before, it was incredible!" How did Rooftops manage to break through to an audience unfamiliar with their sound? They were loud, and the rhythm moved the crowd. "Every song you hear that has a drumbeat that slaps, you just want to move your body to," says Fitchette, "regardless of what style or genre it is. Groove transcends all styles of music."

Having a strong sense of melody helps, too. Our ears aren't trained to follow a melody line that wanders too far in any one direction; this is why many people (besides musicians) are put off by jazz. And since people *feel* rhythm, but follow melody with their ears, good math rock finds the balance between these two things. "You can get as mathy and crazy as you want," sums up Fitchette, "but if I leave the song and I'm not humming it, or whistling the melody, I'm not going to come back to it."

•

The penchant for math rock bands to utilize odd time signatures goes back to the very beginning of the genre. In the late eighties and early nineties, groups such as Slint, Bitch Magnet, and Bastro were all creating something new and complicated. As Scott Tennent writes in his 33 1/3 book about Slint's second LP, *Spiderland*, "The underground had taken a turn from a sloppy, anyone-can-do-it ethos toward something more grandiose, technical, and epic." The building blocks of punk were no longer appealing; musicians wanted to push boundaries and experiment with new forms. Despite not selling many records, and never having anything resembling a hit, an uncommercial group like Sonic Youth was seen as a new type of rock star by rebellious musicians. "People were making interesting music that didn't have to worry about getting on the radio," says Jon Fine. Of course, at the same time, grunge was ascendant and would soon to be king. Nirvana made millions of dollars, sold boatloads of records, and conquered the world, and they did it by speeding up Boston riffs and trashing their gear. Not everyone wanted to join them.

In Pennsylvania, Don Caballero was making another decision that would have a profound effect on math rock: writing songs in odd time signatures. "At the time," recalls drummer Damon Che, "Ian [Williams] was the most interested in introducing time signatures into our little world of underground Pittsburgh music." Williams had been exposed to the concept a few years before when he was drumming for the band Sludgehammer. Even though his first instrument was guitar, the band needed a drummer. Although still a teenager at the time, Williams figured, "How hard could it be?" He took a few lessons from a local session player and jazz musician named Greg Humphries. Humphries was the son of noted jazz drummer Roger Humphries, an influential and respected musician who'd played in numerous bands and traveled the world. In addition to teaching the basics of drumming, Greg Humphries introduced to Williams the idea of odd time signatures. Years later, when he joined Don Cab, Williams brought the concept to his new group. The idea wasn't completely out of left field. "You grow up in the generation where punk rock was the tool to do what you wanted to do," says Williams, "so you're kind of influenced by Black Flag but, at the same time, you had heard Rush and King Crimson."

Even though Che didn't have much experience playing to odd time signatures, he was such a naturally gifted musician he could handle whatever Williams threw his way. Not that the band, at first, thought that it was right thing to do. When they began to use odd time signatures, Williams remembers looking at the band's other guitarist, Mike Banfield; they both kind of rolled their eyes as if to say, "Are we really going to do this?"

They didn't stop there. No lyrics meant no verses or repeated choruses, but the band also avoided any semblance of a discernable song structure. Instead, the group constructed tunes by placing and pasting incongruous parts next to each other with the idea of the drama and shifts between those parts creating tension and interesting sorts of audio jump cuts. "Ian's idea was to make whole songs out of sections that repeat," says Che, "like all music repeats, only each one of our bars is going to sound like when a record skips."

Williams wanted to play with the actual fabric of the music, the bricks and mortar of how it all fits together to make a song. "I'm into patterns," he says. "I've always enjoyed playing patterns, and then fucking those patterns up." Part of his passion was conceptual. In an art history class at college, he'd learned about the Modernists, a group of painters who embraced the flatness of the canvas and dispelled with any attempts to realistically portray life. Instead, pictures were filled with abstract shapes, colors, lines. Paint was just paint. Williams wanted something similar, sound that was just sound. It was also his way of kicking against the notion of the put-upon grunge rocker or moody Gen Xer that was prevalent at the time. "I was into that idea of it just being the sound, and not about a feeling of angst or whatever tortured life Kurt Cobain or Eddie Vedder was supposed to be living at the time."

One of the things that made writing songs like this possible was using a looping pedal to stack several different guitar parts of top of each other. The pedal was first used more out of necessity than creativity. After releasing sophomore record *Don Caballero 2* in 1995, the band took an extended break. In the years that followed, an audience had formed who wanted to see the group play live, so shows were booked. Before the tour started, Mike Banfield left the band, jeopardizing the run of upcoming dates. How could Don Cab play songs they'd recorded as a quartet with three guys? After bass player Eric Emm had begun to use a simple sampler that let him repeat one note for just a second, Williams hit upon the idea of using a looping pedal to reproduce Banfield's parts. He reached out to Tortoise's John McEntire and asked what the best loop pedal was to buy. McEntire sent over an article from *Sound on Sound* magazine. The Akai Headrush was the one to get. "Because of that pedal," Che said in a YouTube interview, "Ian was able to make these amazing loops, and I was a good enough of a drummer to play along to them, and we were able to work as a team." Not only was the tour—and the band—saved, but they also began to use the Headrush to write new material. Williams would record a loop, and the three would jam over it. "It was really quick and intuitive to me," says Williams, "and right then we started writing the songs that would become *American Don*."

A contemporary math rock band who uses loops extensively, live and on record, is Giraffes? Giraffes! Guitarist Joe Andreoli started out with an Akai Headrush, the same as Williams, before graduating to a Boss RC-20, a two-pedal loop station designed for live performance. "It changed how I thought about songs," Andreoli wrote during a *Reddit* "Ask Me Anything" session in 2018. "If I had to choose just one type of pedal to have forever, it'd be a looper." He's gone so far as to say the pedal "changed my life." Andreoli eventually worked his way up to a Boss RC-300, a huge unit containing half a dozen pedals. Whereas the sampler Eric Emm first brought to Don Cab could capture just a second of audio, the RC-300 can record up to three hours. Andreoli utilizes loops on just about every Giraffes? Giraffes! track.

Another two-piece band who made good use of a loop pedal were Foster Parents. A couple of English transplants living in China, they used a looper to lay down rhythm tracks and then build layers on top. In a live situation, this meant they could play anything off their pair of records with just guitar, drums, and loops. Not that it was easy. "There can be a lot of tap dancing involved to start, stop, and clear the loops," says guitarist Gregor Fair, "but that's half of the performance, and half of the fun! Stressful though." They came to rely on looping pedals so much that Fair says now, "We couldn't play a single song, even half of one, without a looper."

No matter how songs are written, rehearsed, or played in front of a crowd, they need to be remembered. Because long and complicated tunes are easy to get lost in, math rock musicians and bands have come up with ways to memorize parts and cues. "My biggest tool is visualization," says Piglet drummer Matthew Parrish.

> I would do it a lot with skateboarding, too. If there was a specific beat or fill that I had in my head, I would try to hear that while visualizing what my limbs would need to do to play it, and that sort of created these pathways that connected what I was hearing to physically executing it. So, I'm able sit at work all day seeing and hearing myself play something and then, when I get to practice, I've pretty much got it.

All the tempo shifts and odd time signatures complicated matters. "The hardest part was learning to count while playing," recalls Cuzco guitarist Will Schoonmaker. "I remember standing in front of Cuzco's other guitarist, Arman Serdarević, and counting with my fingers so he could watch when the 'one' came around again to begin the riff over." Over time, the band would practice enough so that everyone built up the requisite muscle memory, and the musicians no longer had to count in their heads.

Another thing that makes this music difficult to write and remember is that a lot of these songs are created by just two people. Whereas, in the rock world, groups like The White Stripes or The Black Keys are seen as either a novelty or an extreme artistic decision, in math rock having just a drummer and a guitarist is extremely common. Bands such as Hella, Giraffes? Giraffes!, Foster Parents, Cleft, Foco, Pajama Day, and Floral are just a few of many math rock duos who exist today or who have recorded and played live in the past. In a review of Floral's debut album, *The Math Rock Times* wrote, "Two-piece bands have to be on point and more adept to compete with other bands who can have more sound with less effort by any one member." What could be easily seen as a hindrance quickly leads to a wild sort of freedom. "Only got two members?" asks Gregor Fair from Foster Parents. "No problem, just make it more complex. Can't sing? Vocals just detract from the complexity of the guitar work. Don't know how to finish the song? Just go wildly in the other direction and finish with some dissonance." The limitation of having so few players invites an excess of ideas rather than a dearth of them. "The constraints allow you to exceed yourself," wrote novelist Jonathan Safran Foer in an appreciation of the poet Paul Mauldoon. "You are taken to a place you wouldn't have chosen, had you been unconstrained." Whether it's two-piece bands, or the various elements with which math rock is written—odd time signatures, tempo shifts, loops, and so on—what seem like boundaries encourages the genre to be boundless. Writes Foer, "The handcuffs are also the keys to the handcuffs."

•

Another element that plays an important part in writing math rock is alternate tunings. Most guitars are tuned to what's known as "standard" tuning, in which the strings are tuned from low to high. Guitars have been tuned this way for centuries. In an alternate tuning, each string is tuned to a different note. In some alternate tunings, all six strings are tuned so that—when strummed, even without having any fingers on the fretboard—the strings make a chord. For example, a guitar tuned to FACGCE will give you an F major 9 chord just by strumming the open strings. The most common alternate tuning is drop D since it's also one of the simplest; all that needs to be done is tune the low E string down one step. Often used by metal bands to beef up riffs, it was utilized a ton in the nineties by grunge groups such as Soundgarden and Nirvana. Alternate tunings have also been widely used for years in folk, blues, rock, and heavy metal.

Playing in an alternate tuning is a great way for a guitarist to get out of their comfort zone. After years of playing, fingers tend to make the same shapes over and over. By employing alternate tunings, notes, scales, and chords take on new tones and shades. It can free the imagination of an inquisitive player, but it's also a lot of work because it means having to learn new chord shapes and voicings. "Alternate tunings can be helpful to springboard the writing process into a new explorative territory," says Pretend guitarist Tim Ramirez, "similar to playing a different instrument. Each tuning feels very different and makes it difficult to fall into muscle memory habits of standard tunings."

Alternate tunings took hold in the world of math rock with the help of the slow burn success of the debut album from Mike Kinsella's group American Football. Almost all the record's nine songs are in a different tuning. "Every time I picked up a guitar," Kinsella told the *Miami New Times* in 2018, "I'd write a song in whatever tuning it was in when I picked it up." Kinsella was inspired to explore alternate tunings thanks to Cap'n Jazz's Victor Villareal, who would often play in open F tuning. One of the things that makes American Football songs sound so interesting is the fact that Kinsella and second guitarist Steve Holmes play in different tunings. This means that not only are neither in standard tuning, but they're also in alternate tunings *from each other*. On what's become the band's most popular song, "Never Meant," Kinsella's guitar is tuned E-B-B-G#-B-E while Holmes's is G#-B-F#-B-D#. All those different tunings can make playing live difficult. Set lists have not only the name of the songs but also the tunings (making the huge sheets of paper look like alphabet soup). In the early days of the band, this meant lots and lots of time spent between songs tuning. Today, they have guitar techs to help.

As with time signatures, many players who write in alternate tunings don't even know what those tunings are. "Usually, I'll just be fooling around on a guitar and come up with a riff I like," Kinsella told Greg Henkin in 2011, "and then have to figure out what tuning the guitar was in after the fact." Many of those tunings, such as FACGCE, DGCGAC, and DADGAD, have become commonplace in math rock. They're a great way of adding color and variety to a song. However, alternate tunings add yet an additional layer of complexity to a genre which is already known for being difficult.

That difficulty can often start before a person hears even one note of a tune. Just staring at a list of math rock tracks on a record jacket, or as part of a Spotify playlist, and you're already lost. The names are usually long, inscrutable, and have no contextual relationship to the song itself. They're not taken from lyrics (because there usually aren't any lyrics) and, if they're not references to movies or TV shows (Tera Melos *really* loves *The Simpsons*), they're often lengthy and absurd non sequiturs (e.g., TTNG's "It's Not True Rufus, Don't Listen To The Hat"). Don Caballero helped create the template by giving tracks names like, "No One Gives A Hoot About Faux-Ass Nonsense" and "Let's Face It Pal, You Didn't Need That Eye Surgery." And even though math rock titles are usually just plain odd, they're more often funny. Alpha Male Tea Party's "I Haven't Had A Lunch Break Since Windows Vista Came Out" always makes me chuckle, and A Minor Forest's "So Jesus Was At The Last Supper" makes sense in an absurd sort of way. Short-lived Chicago math rock group Dakota/Dakota only released one record, 2003's *Shoot in the Dark*, but every one of its ten songs have hilariously enigmatic names that read like jokes. Steven Wright could recite the back of the CD in a nightclub and get laughs from pretty much each track: "No Matter How Hard I Try, I Never Remember The Alamo," "Misery Loves Company But Hates Hosting," "Getting Angry Is The Worst Way To Prove You're Not Drunk."

These titles do a few things well. First, they fill up the space left free due to the void of lyrics. The song can't "say" anything for itself, because it's instrumental, so the titles can be a proxy for any message the band might want to deliver. They're often also a good match for the music because the length and density of the title becomes a signifier for the tracks themselves; complex songs require complex titles.

This was partially based on what groups had done in the past. In the post-punk and new wave era, bands often had long and nonsensical titles (e.g., Blam Blam Blam's "Don't Fight It Marsha, It's Bigger Than Both Of Us"). Before that, the psychedelic and fantasy overtones of prog made for some truly surreal track names. Quiet Sun's ironically named 1975 LP *Mainstream* featured a chaotic six-minute instrumental titled "Mummy Was An Asteroid, Daddy Was A Small Non-Stick Kitchen Utensil."

Some math rock groups take this to the extreme. In 2018, duo Giraffes? Giraffes! released an almost entirely instrumental concept record entitled *Memory Lame* (yes, puns also make the occasional appearance). The album features thirty-seven songs snippets, or "chapters," some of which are as short as twelve seconds. The story is told from the point of view of a person on a beach who's fallen and hit their head. As they slowly bleed to death, they're visited by various visions and recollections. "It's an album about the mind and about your memories and truth versus fiction," guitarist Joe Andreoli told *Music Radar* shortly after the record came out. Much of the album, reflecting the experience of what the protagonist is going through, is random and chaotic, notes and phrases coming at you like shards of memories or half-remembered sensations. The titles reinforce this impression: "Chapter 14: I Am An Electronic Device Skipping Across The Pavement And Flipping Fucking Wild Into The Woods," "Chapter 34: HOLY! HOLY! HOLY! HOLY! HOLY! HOLY! HOLY! HOLY! HOLY! HOLY! HOLY! HOLY! HOLY! HOLY!" Listening to the record in one sitting, as the band intended (Giraffes? Giraffes! initially delivered the LP to their label as a continuous, forty-one-minute track) indeed feels like a complete journey and experience. By the time the last song arrives, "At The Turf Field Behind My Parents' House," both protagonist and listener have reached some sort of conclusion; the record, and a life, have come to an end. It's heady and brilliant stuff, showing that math rock bands can push language just as far as they push music.

Not all math rock bands do this. Some go in the opposite direction, trading long and wordy titles for short and simple ones. TTNG (back when they were still known as This Town Needs Guns) had a record called *Animals* where each track was, you guessed it, named after an animal (first five tracks: "Pig," "Baboon," "Panda," "Gibbon," "Rabbit"). The group Standards goes even farther, embracing a kind of Day-Glo aesthetic across their entire catalog. Albums feature cartoonish drawings of fruit, and almost all their songs are named after produce ("Strawberry," "Melon," "Mango"). Meanwhile, records have been named *Fruit Town* and *Fruit Island*. Other bands have simplified this even further; each of American Football's three albums are named *American Football*.

One of my all-time favorite math rock titles is "In the Absence of Strong Evidence to the Contrary, One May Step Out of the Way of the Charging Bull," from Don Cab's third LP *What Burns Never Returns*. I love the name of this song because it sums up everything about the genre. You're not supposed to stand in the way of things that can kill you. To do so is dangerous, tantamount to suicide. And yet, ironically, taking chances and facing death can make you feel alive. You're also not supposed to write songs in odd time signatures and alternate tunings, where the tempo changes and no two parts seem to match the next. The easiest thing in the world is to get out of the way of the bull. Another easy thing to do is write three-minute pop songs. But where's the fun in that?

6 Tremolo + Delay: Playing Math Rock

The first issue of UK punk zine *Sideburns*, which hit the streets in January 1977, contains one of the genre's most potent and well-known images. Editor Tony Moon, faced with blank space on the second page, filled it with drawings of three basic guitar chords (an open A, E, and G). Next to each diagram, in capital letters, he wrote, THIS IS A CHORD, THIS IS ANOTHER, THIS IS A THIRD. At the bottom was scrawled and underlined, NOW FORM A BAND. Hundreds of disaffected English youths would soon take Moon's advice to heart, forming punk groups and getting on stages all around the country clutching instruments they could barely play. Bands like The Damned and Sex Pistols were following in the footsteps of New Yorkers The Ramones, whose first record had come out the year before and featured primitive but effective playing. Songs were short, fast, and full of attitude. Anyone could make this music, and anyone did. In just a few short months, a whole scene was created.

Playing math rock not only involves many, many more chords than the three Moon provided, it also requires dozens of advanced techniques. In punk, all a drummer must do is pound a relentless 4/4 beat. The songs are so fast there isn't any space for things like fills or complicated patterns. Contrast this with math rock, where drums are very much in the foreground and tunes are rarely played in common time. In Toe, Kashikura Takashi's drums give most of the group's songs their distinctive sound and feel. In Jon Fine's book *Your Band Sucks,* he writes, "the drummer must be both caveman and mathematician." Punk drummers usually hew much closer to cavemen than mathematicians (in both their playing and general look and demeanor). Punk guitarists, meanwhile, play only a small variety of chords while their right hands chug away relentlessly like a piston with rapid fire downstrokes. No solos, no filler, no showing off. As Lene Cortina wrote on *Punk Diaries* in 2018, in a post praising Tony Moon's graphic of the three chords, "Music doesn't have to be fancy or complicated, sometimes it just has to be easy to get to grips with."

Math rock might not fit the description of "fancy," but it certainly is complicated. In an ironic situation that's basically a reverse of what happened in London in 1977, math rock's birth was partly a reaction against the back-to-basics indie and alternative rock music scenes of the nineties. Alternative rock, as evidenced by its name, was meant to be an "alternative" to the glossy and lightweight bands then taking up space on the pop charts and MTV. Hair metal had watered down the thrash and hardcore scenes, and Guns N' Roses were the biggest rock group in the world. With the advent of grunge, bands like Nirvana and Pearl Jam sold millions of records with a sound that was big on grit and attitude, but short on complexity. Within the smaller world of indie rock, the primitivism of bands and performers like Beat Happening, Half Japanese, and Daniel Johnston, showed you could get by with just one or two of the chords Moon supplied punk bands.

Having musical chops at the dawn of the nineties was as big a sin as having them toward the end of the seventies. When polarizing alternative rock group Smashing Pumpkins started making ambitious albums partly inspired by second-wave prog heroes Rush, indie rockers quickly and openly mocked them for it. California slackers Pavement dissed the band in their song "Range Life," and few people took the Pumpkins' side. The rise of math rock slowly began to turn the tide. Don Caballero, Bastro, and Tortoise showed that you could make complex, complicated, and challenging music, and yet still retain street cred and draw a crowd at the Lounge Ax or Empty Bottle on a Friday night. Like the heyday of prog, where many of the musicians were classically trained, members of math rock bands over the years would have degrees in music theory or composition, and the music they created showed it. Chops were back.

One of the most prevalent, and difficult, techniques used to play math rock is tapping. Tapping is the result of guitarists playing notes with both hands on the fretboard via a combination of hammer-ons and pull-offs. A hammer-on is when a player creates a note by quickly bringing down a finger of their fretting hand onto a string to sound a note. A pull-off is the opposite; the player creates a note when they lift their finger from a string (this is done either with just the tip of their finger or a fingernail). Both techniques had been around for hundreds of years before folk music legend Pete Seeger coined the terms "pull-off" and "hammer-on" in his chapbook *How to Play the 5-String Banjo*, which he self-released in 1948. Hammer-ons and pull-offs, performed on their own with just the fretting hand, can be easily mastered by intermediate players. Tapping is trickier since it involves both hands working at once. The technique is appealing to guitarists because it allows them to play more quickly and to strike more notes. In essence, what the player is doing is gaining an extra hand, since the picking hand can now also play notes on the fretboard.

An early practitioner of tapping was Roy Smeck. Known as the "Wizard of the Strings," Smeck was proficient on guitar, banjo, and ukulele. Through his constant touring on the vaudeville circuit, and then appearing in films in the twenties and thirties (including some of the first sound films ever), he even helped popularize the instruments. Tapping was a big part of his act and his playing. A few decades later, Jimmie Webster devised a method for playing guitar using nothing but tapping. Webster hoped his Touch System would catch on as an entirely new way of playing the instrument. Webster's method amounted to basically playing piano on the guitar: the left hand tapped chords, while the right tapped melodies; all eight fingers were utilized. Webster tried to spread the gospel of tapping via records, like his 1959 album *Webster's Unabridged*. He even worked with Gretsch to make guitars aimed at potential Touch System players.

Despite Webster's Touch System technique never quite catching on, several "touch guitars" were later developed and manufactured that were intended exclusively for double-handed tapping. In 1961, a double-necked instrument called the DuoLectar was introduced. The single-neck Chapman Stick followed a bit more than a decade later. More recent inventions include the Warr Guitar (favored by mathcore band Behold The Arctopus) and the Megatar. The Megatar is a beast featuring a dozen individual strings, six tuned like a guitar and six like a bass, the idea being that one person can basically play the role of both a guitarist and bassist at the same time. Before going out of business in 1999, Megatar's slogan was "12 Strings, 2 Hands, No Limits."

Double-handed tapping on a standard electric guitar was introduced to rock audiences by Genesis's Steve Hackett, who stumbled onto the technique. "I was trying to play a tiny phrase from Toccata and Fugue by Bach," he told *Music Radar* in 2012, "and I was wondering how to do it, because you couldn't really do it across the strings. I figured that if I could do it on one string, then I'd be using the fretboard like a keyboard." Hackett tapped on several Genesis albums, starting with 1971's *Nursery Cryme*, where the technique appeared in the solo to "The Musical Box" and in the intro for "The Return of the Giant Hogweed." Eddie Van Halen would later put tapping to great effect in several songs, most notably "Eruption" from the band's 1978 debut. Later, rock guitarists like Randy Rhoads, Steve Vai, and Paul Gilbert all began to develop tapping techniques, as did jazz players like Stanley Jordan.

•

In Pennsylvania, Don Caballero's Ian Williams was unaware of virtuosos like Jordan, having only been exposed to tapping through heavy metal guitarists like Eddie Van Halen. The technique seemed to him like a ripe area to explore, and a way to stake out his own territory, make his own statement. Williams, still a young guy at the time—barely into his twenties—was forming his sense of himself and figuring out what he wanted his musical identity to be. Sonic Youth had left a huge imprint on the underground rock scene, and Williams saw that too many bands in the nineties were simply aping what the New York noise group had already done in the eighties. Williams didn't want to be yet another. Tapping also meant he could bring to his guitar playing what jazz musician Greg Humphries had taught him about drums. "I do think it influenced the way I saw playing the guitar," says Williams of his experience as a drummer. "Two drumsticks, two hands attacking the strings. When I finally started playing guitar again after Sludgehammer, I was a better guitar player. I was more equipped to think of things in rhythmic terms."

The way Williams used tapping was different from thrash or metal guitarists. Instead of soloing, or using the technique to merely play fast, Williams worked his fingers on the fretboard like cogs in a machine.

> The tapping I did a lot of times was three fingers on the right hand playing three different notes, and two fingers on the left hand playing two different notes. And I would cycle through each finger or note. Therefore, the pattern was three against two, which would cycle around differently each time. So, the left hand went back and forth on a 1-2 pattern and the right hand went 1-2-3, independently of each other.

And even though using both hands meant there was a temptation to play in even time signatures, Williams avoided this by creating uneven combinations. "With fingers it was a way of getting beyond the two-foot sway thing. Three or five or whatever. And then the signatures could kind of disturb the fabric, or complacent pattern." And whereas Eddie Van Halen did everything he could to hide his technique, going so far as to turn his back on audiences so that his tapping would be kept secret, Williams was always front and center, tapping his heart out while also chewing gum and blowing bubbles. "It was very transparent," he says. "You could see what I was doing. So, if you didn't grow up taking guitar lessons, or learning how to play guitar licks, it was a way into the guitar for people who didn't have to learn the rock and roll canon first."

One of the people who took notice of Williams's tapping was singer/songwriter Marnie Stern. She told *The Washington Post* in 2013 that it was watching Don Cab videos that introduced her to the technique. "I saw a few seconds and noticed Ian had both hands on the neck of his guitar. Then I started fiddling around doing it, not really knowing what I was doing." Stern's gone on to release five math rock adjacent records for indie rock labels, and she's recorded and toured with luminaries from the scene such as Hella's Zach Hill and Tera Melos's Vince Rogers.

One of the new breed of math rock guitarists to make tapping a central part of their playing arsenal is Covet's Yvette Young. Covet was formed in the Bay area by Young a decade ago and has quickly become one of the most important bands on the math rock scene. Young was born and raised in San Jose to Chinese immigrants who'd moved from Beijing to achieve the American Dream (her mom was a dancer, her father a composer and accordion player). They started her on music lessons at an early age: piano at four, violin at seven. When she was nine, Young began to play piano competitively. This would continue, with recitals every couple of months, for almost ten years. The schedule was grueling, the competition fierce; Young's parents pushed her to be the best. After she tripped and broke her pinkie, Young had to quickly resume practicing for an upcoming recital. The broken bone didn't have time to properly heal. Today, the finger is bent slightly and sometime locks up when she's playing live.

The pressure to perform (not to mention win), in addition to her schoolwork and her own penchant for perfectionism, made Young increasingly miserable. She hated practicing four hours a day and being told the "right" way to play a piece. In middle school she developed an eating disorder which eventually landed her in the hospital. While recuperating, she taught herself to play guitar. The first song she figured out by ear was "Six Feet From the Edge" by Creed. She was soon playing Radiohead covers and, inspired by American Football, dabbling in alternate tunings. Learning the instrument allowed her to discover a love of music on her own terms.

After graduating early from UCLA with a fine art degree (Young's also an accomplished artist who paints and draws), she formed Covet with bassist David Adamiak and drummer Keith Grimshaw. They opened for fellow math rock bands CHON and Tera Melos, as well as progressive metal powerhouse Polyphia. Covet self-released their first EP in 2015 before signing to Triple Crown for their debut album, 2018's *Effloresce*. A second album, *Technicolor,* followed in 2020, with third LP *Catharsis* being released in 2023.

Young's super technical and melodic style features a lot of tapping. She came to the technique out of necessity. "I started out writing music as a solo guitar player just in my bedroom, and I didn't have a band at the time," Young told Lee Anderton in a 2019 YouTube interview. "So I had to think about, 'How do I sound as full as possible with just one person? How do I give the illusion that there's a bass part going on?' Tapping is a really great way to achieve that."

Even though Young utilizes tapping in almost each Covet song, she's made sure to develop a wide array of skills. "Technique is like basically your arsenal of tools. And I feel like, as an artist, you want the biggest toolkit possible so that you can translate all your ideas most effectively." This means not overly relying on any one approach.

> You don't want to use all your tools at once in the song, because it can sound kind of cluttered. So, for me, technique is only as valuable as how much it serves what you're trying to convey. So, if I need to do like a crazy tap run, I'll do it because that's what I wanted for that section. That's the only way I can play what I hear in my head.

Other prominent math rock guitarists who make extensive use of tapping are Tim Collis from TTNG, Marcos Mena from Standards, Nick Reinhart from Tera Melos, and Brock Benzel from Invalids.

As vital and prevalent as tapping is in math rock, it's just one of several techniques employed by guitarists in the genre. Other techniques include alternate picking, finger picking, and hybrid picking. Alternate picking is simply picking in an up and down pattern; this allows players to play a rapid succession of notes. Finger picking is using one's fingertips to pluck the strings. This has been a mainstay in folk, country, and bluegrass for years. Hybrid picking, as the name suggests, allows a player to use a pick and fingers at the same time. It's a great solution for the player who wants to take advantage of tapping and finger picking but isn't quite ready to completely give up playing with a pick.

•

Beyond how instruments are played, a crucial aspect in math rock is how they *sound*. Drummers opt for crisp hits that lean more towards the snap of jazz than the god of thunder style of hard rock, while guitarists aim for a bright, crystal-clear tone. Many math rock guitarists achieve that twinkly timbre by playing a Fender Telecaster, a product that first hit the market in 1950. Back then it was known as the Broadcaster. Leo Fender changed the name in 1951 after Gretsch complained that it was too similar to their own Broadkaster. Telecasters were an instant hit with players, especially country musicians who loved its silvery and twangy accents. It's remained both a popular guitar, and largely unchanged, since its introduction more than half a century ago. Famous Telecaster players over the years have included Keith Richards, Bruce Springsteen, and Radiohead's Jonny Greenwood.

Telecaster's glimmery sound comes from two sources: the wood it's made from (it has an alder body and maple neck) and the narrow, single coil pickup located close to the bridge. This combination gives the guitar a sparkly, trebly intonation (as opposed to the thick and beefy sound produced via Les Paul's mahogany body and wide humbucker pickups). The complex music of math rock begs for the transparent tones of a Tele. Whereas the guitar sound of other genres, like metal or thrash, is all about creating huge swarms of noise with the intent to bludgeon the listener, math rock demands purity and clarity. Why play all those notes if no one can hear them?

"The relationship between what we call 'math rock' and the Fender Telecaster is not unlike the symbiosis found between a good bag of chips and the perfect jar of salsa," Michael Whiteside wrote on *Fecking Bahamas* in 2019. "While fully flavorful on their own, when combined, the results are often a profoundly addictive and rarely challenged combination."

The genre's obsession with Telecasters was cemented with American Football's influential debut record. The vivid and bright notes of Mike Kinsella's and Steve Holmes's Telecasters, recorded with few pedals or effects, have ended up having a strong and lasting influence on the genre. Math rock guitarists continue to seek out Telecasters to produce interesting tones. "I always thought it'd be really cool if a guitar could sound like raindrops," says Pretend guitarist Tim Ramirez, "and I suppose I figured a Telecaster was equipped to produce a sound like that. I got a Telecaster early on and played it throughout. Its shimmery essence and tendency to produce a softer tone when fingerpicking was ideal to me."

Whereas Dinosaur Jr.'s J. Mascis or My Bloody Valentine's Kevin Shields derive a lot of their saturated, overdriven sound from Fender Jazzmasters and a floor full of pedals, most math rock guitarists who play Telecasters prefer to keep their signal almost completely dry. All you're likely to hear on a Tele is a bit of tremolo and delay (as evidenced by the Toe song "Tremolo + Delay"). Washington band Rooftops was so enamored with a clean sound, as well as with tapping, that the group's motto was, "No picks, no pedals, no problem."

Bass players follow many of the same techniques as six string guitarists. In Don Cab, you'd often see bassist Eric Emm tapping alongside Ian Williams. Drummers are similarly free to break out of the standard rock styles of playing. Since there's no verse-chorus-verse structure, drummers are liberated from just keeping the beat or locking in with the bass player to establish a groove. With their traditional roles as timekeepers removed, math rock drummers like Toe's Kashikura Takashi and Don Cab's Damon Che are free to comment on the music—through their drum parts—rather than merely accompany it. They play inside and outside and all around the notes and chords and melodies. And since many math rock songs are in odd time signatures, the beat is always changing and dynamic. The goal then becomes less about getting people to *move* than it is to get them to *feel*.

Che would make use of the space provided by inserting into sections what he calls "off pocket bombs," meaning extra beats here and there. He was inspired to do this by Gang of Four's Hugo Burnham and jazz great Elvin Jones. Whereas Jones used those accents in a cruising, walking sort of jazz context, Burnham—in songs like "Why Theory" or "If I Could Keep it All For Myself"—would throw in a hit on the floor tom to knock the listener off balance. These eccentric and literally off-beat bursts are great for bringing emphasis to a part. Kenneth Topham from Giraffes? Giraffes! often does something similar. As he told *The Math Rock Times* in 2018, "I like to sneak an extra beat into spots. Just like a hidden thing that flips the beat so if you're nodding your head along on the downbeat, you suddenly find yourself nodding on the upbeat." All those hidden touches, played on both guitars and drums, give math rock its distinctive sound and mood.

•

What do all these advanced techniques mean for the run-of-the-mill fan who wants to emulate their heroes by learning how to play their songs? After all, much of the appeal of punk was that anyone could play it. Those three chords Tony Moon scrawled in *Sideburns* could be passably strummed in seconds. Even more complicated fare, like the opening to "Stairway to Heaven" (the rite of passage for generations of suburban would-be rock gods) could be mastered with enough patience by young players with a few lessons under their belts. Does that mean math rock's absurdly high bar of musicianship puts it completely out of range for amateur musicians? Not necessarily.

As a young English teenager, Stephen Hazel listened to contemporary emo and pop punk bands like Get Up Kids, Braid, and At The Drive In. After getting a copy of Tera Melos's 2007 EP *Drugs to the Dear Youth*, the song "40 Rods To The Hog's Head" set off a lightbulb. It was chaotic and noisy, but still had a discernible melody; Stephen had never heard anything like it. He was hooked.

Not content to just be a fan, Stephen wanted to play like the math rock guitarists he was rapidly discovering. At the time, he was studying music in college and taking lessons from a tutor who was in his fifties. Stephen wanted to know how to play "Melody 4" by Tera Melos, a song from their untitled record (the one featuring three headless guys carrying chainsaws on the cover). The track is almost five full minutes of absolutely batshit fast and crazy six-string histrionics. As Stephen played it for his teacher, the man sat there with a shocked look on his face, as if to say, "What the hell is *this*?" At the next lesson, however, the tutor arrived excited at having worked out some of the difficult track. Between his teacher's help, and some online tablature he found for the song, Stephen—after days and days of intense practice—ended up being able to play a portion of the song. Not that it was easy. "I remember thinking," Stephen recalls today, "it took me that long just to learn twenty seconds of the song. How do you even play the rest?!" Proud of being able to play at least part of the tune, Stephen recorded himself on his laptop playing a minute of "Melody 4." He uploaded the video to YouTube, where it received a positive comment from Covet's Yvette Young, just another unknown guitarist at the time. "woooooow.:) this is slick. really nice job."

Despite having spent years mastering many if not all the techniques associated with playing math rock, there's still some stuff even Stephen can't play. Bands like Piglet, Hella, and Tera Melos have so much going on in their chaotic tracks that it can be hard to find the actual notes or dig into what's being played. And when you add in elements like alternate tunings, multiple guitar parts, and recording quality, figuring out how to play a track becomes quite a daunting challenge. But it can be done. "I clearly remember how difficult it was to learn 'Chinchilla' by TTNG many years ago," Stephen says. "There was a lot of new territory to explore on the guitar for me, and I wasn't really versed in using anything other than standard tuning at that point, so I remember that being a challenge that took a month or so to learn. It certainly improved my finger picking technique!" Even when Stephen had stems he could isolate and slow down, it was still a daunting process.

I remember finding Guitar Pro files of parts of math rock songs, and I would highlight a bar in the program and loop it until I could get it at 100% speed. Then the next phrase would be something completely different that doesn't complement, so to speak, the idea before it, so it was quite a time-consuming task just to learn a single section.

The problem wasn't just because some of the parts were played fast. "Most of the time it's not the speed but rather the oddness of the rhythm, the phrasing of the ideas, and so on that make it such a challenge," says Stephen. "Also, because the songs are so unconventional it becomes more of a memorization task rather than learning something that has a clear conventional chord progression and a complementing melody." The technique Ian Williams had come up with to place incongruous parts next to each other to create an odd sensation for the listener tends to wreak havoc for players trying to learn the songs. But Stephen, who has since turned his love of math rock into a successful YouTube channel called Let's Talk About Math Rock, where he provides online lessons and tutorials on how to master the genre, has practical advice for anyone who wishes to learn how to perform the style: "Don't be put off, just set some goals, invest the time into those goals, and you will be able to play the math rock you want to play, no problem."

Musicians who take on the challenge need to also be careful to not overly emphasize the technical aspects of the genre (even though this is easy to do, given how technical the music is). What drove Yvette Young from playing piano competitively was having to adhere to the dogmatic rigidity of the form. She didn't escape from that world only to enter another just like it. To give up the freedom of being liberated from traditional song structures in the name of mechanical proficiency goes against what math rock truly stands for.

Stephen Hazel wanted to learn a bit of that Tera Melos track because he'd felt an emotional and intellectual connection to the music. That it helped him grow as a player was just an added benefit. This is the genius of math rock: it engages both sides of your brain at once. Sure, there's the counting and technique and focusing on the form within the formlessness, but there's also the colors and emotions and shades of the way the music makes you feel. For that emotion to be carried through to the listener, the playing must be human. Sometimes that means making mistakes. "I, personally, am terrified of being included into a category where virtuosity is prized as I am very much not a virtuoso," says Clever Girl saxophonist Duncan Robinson. His bandmate, guitarist James Bailey, agrees. "A lot of math rock bands are super proficient and technical, which isn't us at all." The band chalks up the popularity of their classic EP, *No Drum and Bass in The Jazz Room*, to the fact that the recording is a bit messy. They didn't quantize each note or slavishly match up to a click track. Some of the playing's actually a little sloppy. Instead of trying to make every little thing perfect, they opted for creating an atmosphere and mood. By doing so, they counterintuitively created perfection. That's the point of math rock: To find the spirit and soul inside of this incredibly technical and complex music. It's not easy—in the same way that double-handed tapping isn't easy but it can be done.

7   Here Comes Everybody: The Internet and Math Rock

The invention of the internet had an outsized effect on the music industry. The ease of online ordering, and the rise of sites like Amazon, decimated brick and mortar retail operations. The music industry also never recovered from their fumbled attempts to fend off filesharing at the end of the nineties. On the plus side, it's never been easier for bands and fans to connect, and for musicians to record music (often at home) and make that music available to anyone in the world. All of this has led to a proliferation of artists and genres and created a whole new paradigm around how music is both consumed and discovered.

The first real push the web gave to math rock was the introduction of Myspace in 2003. After the internet became a dominant force in the late nineties, with more people going online thanks to faster connection speeds, a new kind of website began to emerge: the social network. Pioneering companies like GeoCities, Six Degrees, and LiveJournal segued to Friendster and Tribe. By the time Myspace launched, being online had become an interactive experience. Instead of merely clicking on links, people could join groups, share photos, and connect with existing acquaintances (or make new ones). Myspace, which had initially modeled itself as "a place for friends," soon became a huge music discovery engine. Bands created pages, using them to premiere songs, post demos, and promote upcoming tours. In no time, groups and performers like Arctic Monkeys and Janelle Monae parlayed attention on Myspace to score record deals and huge audiences. This was a totally new model that upended decades of pop music tradition.

For a long time, bands and musicians had just two avenues to get popular: play shows or get on the radio. The introduction of MTV in the eighties provided a third option, but videos could be expensive and, after a few maverick years, MTV's daily rotation focused on big hits. Touring, especially in a big country like America, costs money (funds a new or struggling group generally doesn't have). And for bands who renounced current and popular scenes or sounds, getting on the radio, let alone scoring a hit, is difficult if not impossible. Myspace created a new way not only for established groups to gain new fans, but it allowed niche genres and sub-genres to build an audience. In a 2005 *Wired* story called "Bands Embrace Social Networking," Myspace's VP of Marketing, Jamie Kantrowitz, talked about how smaller bands and scenes were using the website to reach new fans: "Indie doesn't get big radio play. So all these bands that are punk and indie have really seen success through Myspace. It's a place to discover new music and for artists to get their music out there."

Given that math rock was more obscure than even punk or indie rock, having a platform where fans around the world could find each other, discover new groups, and connect, was huge. In a *Forbes* article from 2019 entitled "How Myspace Opened the Door to Niche Music Genres," a Myspace employee is quoted on the subject of the website's appeal to devotees of musical styles that flew well under the radar of popular appreciation: "We knew that it was the music that lived in between or outside of genres that would ignite global communities of niche kids who depended on Myspace to find others like them."

In the mid-2000s, Myspace was crucial in connecting, if not just plain creating, a math rock audience. "Myspace was probably the biggest reason that we started a math rock band," says Rooftops guitarist Drew Fitchette, "because that was how we all found those bands at the time." The process went something like this: a person would go to Myspace and friend somebody. Maybe it was a person they knew already from school or around town, or it might be someone they never met who lived halfway across the world. They'd scroll down to see what kind of bands that person had in their music section. Here they might come across alien names like Joan of Arc, Don Caballero, Lite, or Piglet. Most bands had a page on Myspace with four or five songs. If the new listener liked what they heard, they'd go to a record store and buy a CD of the band they'd heard on Myspace. And because math rock groups weren't being written about or featured anywhere else, Myspace became the only place to discover them, not to mention to meet people who also liked them.

It wasn't just about fans finding new music, or bands building an audience. Groups were using the site to locate like-minded bands. This was helpful for scheduling tours as well as creating a general support system. "When we were touring, we'd use Myspace to find local bands," says Fitchette. "You could just search 'math rock LA', and a band like Pretend would pop up. We would message them and be like, 'Hey, we're going to tour this summer and be in LA these two dates. Do you guys want to play shows with us?'" Sometimes these new and random connections led to a group getting signed. After

Rooftops began exchanging emails with Toe, the Japanese band got signed to Topshelf records, Rooftops's label.

In 2005, just two years after it launched, Rupert Murdoch's News Corp bought Myspace for $580 million. The following year, Myspace would be the most visited website on the planet. It was an amazing ride for the brash new company, but it didn't last. A new website named YouTube, introduced the year Myspace was sold, was quickly becoming a place where people were spending lots of time.

The first video uploaded to YouTube was a nineteen-second clip shot at the San Diego Zoo of one of the site's three co-founders, Jawed Karim, talking about elephants. It's not the kind of content that seemed destined to get lots of eyeballs, or strike fear in the heart of Myspace. But that was sort of the point. YouTube was created to be a place where ordinary people could post anything they wanted, for free. By the end of that first year, the site was logging more than two million views a day. Six months later, there were more than twenty-five million videos on YouTube, with 20,000 new videos being added a day. Google, who'd introduced its own video platform (without much success), bought YouTube for $1.65 billion toward the end of 2006, less than two years after its founding. This was an even bigger payday, in a shorter amount of time, than Myspace had experienced.

YouTube began to employ community managers to create categories around subjects like sports and comedy, aggregating clips for the home page. Music, even early in the site's existence, began to be the subject of lots of videos. In 2008, YouTube's community managers (also sometimes called editors) found clips of a young and unknown singer named Justin Bieber covering popular songs. He was only twelve years old at the time. They put him on the home page. Bieber's clips soon attracted the attention of the music industry, who quickly signed him to a major label deal. His career was off and running.

It wasn't just pop stars who were using the platform to their advantage. Two years before Bieber was discovered, an up-and-coming Chicago group named OK Go posted to YouTube a video they'd made for practically nothing for their song "Here It Goes Again." The video featured the four band members, eight treadmills, and some inventive choreography. The charming and homemade video, which the group shot themselves with one camera and no assistance or help from their record label or manager, quickly went viral. It racked up almost a million views on its first day. The song became a hit, the band was asked to reprise the routine on several TV shows, and the video won a Grammy.

More bands, and labels, followed suit, uploading to YouTube music videos and performances. But then a funny thing happened. People started uploading their record collections. Whole records or just single tracks began to appear. The more obscure the better. Sometimes clips were taken down for copyright infringement, but other times they stayed up. Hundreds of songs and then thousands, and then hundreds of thousands. These were then combined by users into long and elaborate playlists and mixes. YouTube was slowly becoming a never-ending digital jukebox, turning on music fans around the world to new bands, performers, eras, and genres they might never have been exposed to. In the pre-internet era, this kind of knowledge and exposure could only be obtained through older siblings, cool neighbors, or that wise old dude down at the record store who seemed to know every band in existence. That information now began to be served up via algorithms that intuited what we wanted before we even knew that we wanted it. Like maybe a video whose thumbnail was a cartoon dinosaur holding a Rubik's Cube. Who in the world could resist clicking on something like that?

•

English group Clever Girl is made up of Sam Weatherald and James Bailey on guitar, Luke Hamilton on drums, Tom Gelber on bass, and Duncan Robinson on sax. When they got together in Sheffield in 2009 they were all in college, apart from Hamilton. Most of them had been in indie groups of varying levels of success, and they each wanted to try something new. Clever Girl was formed to make math rock and jazz-influenced instrumental music in the vein of America's Pele and Canada's Do Make Say Think. Sheffield had been home to some big bands in the past, including The Human League, Pulp and, more recently, Arctic Monkeys. None of them were math rock. The only local group who was doing anything remotely like Clever Girl was King Capisce, a five-piece with two saxophonists who played instrumental jazz. Despite getting a few high-profile gigs, like opening for TTNG when they came through town, most of Clever Girl's handful of shows were performed to friends. People clapped, were politely enthusiastic, but the lingering question seemed to be, "So, when are these guys going to get a singer?"

In 2010 the band quickly recorded an EP, *No Drum and Bass in the Jazz Room*, and uploaded it to Myspace (the title is a reference to Weatherald's bedroom). They let people download it for free, but accepted donations. There weren't many. The page still exists (myspace.com/clevergirllovesyou), and even though the embedded music player no longer works, the group's stats remain. "Teleblister" had the most listens at just over 1,700 while "Sleepyhead Symphony" never managed to crack a thousand. A decade later, these songs would log millions of plays on a variety of websites and platforms.

After the EP was released, the members of Clever Girl went their separate ways. Literally. One moved to Japan, another to Colombia. They got jobs, got married, started families. Before that happened, however, there was a brief discussion about staying together and making a go of the group. They decided against it. They hadn't made any money up to this point, so why think it'd be any different in the future? That was the end of Clever Girl. Until it wasn't.

The name had come from Steven Spielberg's original *Jurassic Park* film, which came out in 1993. The movie looms large in the lives of Clever Girl's members, having come out when they were just kids. Sam Weatherald was obsessed with dinosaurs at the time, and still remembers seeing the film with his dad (and being terrified the entire time). In the film, park official Robert Muldoon, impressed at the intelligence of the dinosaur who has just outsmarted him, mumbles, "clever girl." There's also the famous scene where scientist Jeff Goldblum lectures park owner Richard Attenborough on his hubris for playing God. "Life breaks free," Goldblum explains, "it expands to new territories and crashes through barriers." The gathered scientists do their best to assure Goldblum there's no danger, that they'll be able to control the dinosaurs. Goldblum remains unconvinced. "Life," he somberly announces, "uh, finds a way."

A few years after Clever Girl uploaded *No Drum and Bass* to Myspace, a fan took the files and uploaded them to YouTube. Since the EP never had a physical release, and thus no official cover, the fan used some *Jurassic Park*-inspired art the band had used briefly as their profile photo on Facebook. The cartoon graphic of a dinosaur solving a Rubik's Cube, with the words CLEVER GIRL in the *Jurassic Park* font, had been downloaded from a website that puts pop culture images on T-shirts, mugs, and mousepads. Slowly but surely, the YouTube version began to get views. Lots of views. Tens of thousands, then hundreds of thousands. It was inching toward a million when it was taken down for copyright infringement. The band hadn't played a part in any of it. The video was taken down due to other music the uploader had put online. The group hadn't minded the songs being on YouTube. They'd been watching it all happen, bemused and slightly bewildered. By now they'd also put the files on Bandcamp, using as an ad hoc cover a photo Weatherald had taken of a sunset from his childhood home. They got lots of downloads, as well as people from all around the world sending them nice comments (e.g., "I took 2.5 tabs of acid and this changed my life"). The songs were then added to Spotify, where they increasingly came up next to tracks by bands like Covet, Piglet, and TTNG (the group Clever Girl had opened for all those years ago). Math rock fans on Reddit championed the album, giving it thousands of upvotes. The EP even got uploaded yet again to YouTube, where it began to rack up hits. It has since hit a million views.

Sensing that all these plays were the result of more than just algorithm bait, the band decided to press up some vinyl copies. This meant the EP finally got an official cover. Friend of the band Greg Hartley designed a beautiful sleeve of a young girl in coveralls surrounded by sunflowers holding up a Rubik's Cube while riding a dinosaur. It was a perfect homage to the cartoon graphic fans of the record had come to associate with the band. With a physical artifact available, the group felt this was going to be the real test. It was one thing to listen to the EP on YouTube, where all you had to do was click past a few annoying ads, but it was something else altogether to shell out twenty bucks for the real thing. People did. The first pressing sold out quickly, followed by a second and a third. Copies are now selling for hundreds of dollars on Discogs.

Clever Girl wasn't the only math rock band this happened to. The first group associated with the genre to be given an afterlife thanks to the internet was Slint. The four-piece from Louisville, Kentucky, recorded one proper album for Touch and Go and broke up before the LP even came out. There were no videos, no tour, no interviews. Just six songs and an enigmatic black and white cover. Released in 1991, *Spiderland* barely made waves even in indie rock circles. At the time, there was no math rock, post-rock, or instrumental rock scenes. So, other than a few tastemakers like Steve Albini (who declared the album "flawless"), there were no like-minded bands to champion or sing Slint's praises. *Spiderland* sank like a stone. Until constant word of mouth and the internet slowly brought it back to life. In a story entitled "The Band That the Internet Remembered," writer Samuel Hyland talks about stumbling onto Slint at four in the morning as part of a Spotify math rock playlist. "I was more scared than enticed." He took the plunge, and a new world opened before him. One that had a deep and immediate impact. "The knowledge is in your hands now—and you can't unsee, unhear, nor undiscover what you got yourself into." Heralded now as a classic album and ground zero for math rock, *Spiderland* would have been forgotten had it not been for the web. "Slint is really one of the first bands to become popular and have a career resurgence," wrote William Covert on *Fecking Bahamas* in 2016, "due to the internet and their profound influence on contemporary bands."

Chicago group Piglet, the same as Clever Girl, put out just an EP and then went their separate ways. That should have been the end. Instead, it was just the beginning. The band's reputation slowly grew, and they began to be held up as one of the pinnacles of the growing genre, all because of one EP. "It just didn't seem to want to die," says drummer Matthew Parrish. After watching interest in *Lava Land* grow for years, the band funded a vinyl release using Kickstarter. It has been reissued a few times since, with all editions selling out quickly. "It's been really amazing and touching to me," says Parrish. "Piglet is so much bigger than the sum of its parts at this point. It's kinda like we had this baby and raised it, and now it functions and contributes to the world totally independent of our influence."

Back when Clever Girl's *No Drum and Bass* was first being given away for free on Myspace, the band made a long post on Facebook telling friends and followers about the record. The message ended with a prediction, and a request, both of which were made more or less in jest:

> of course we're hoping that off the back of this EP we'll become post-humously bigger than Keane, and one day there will be a 'bring back whispa' style facebook campaign and due to public demand clever girl will reunite and arise once more to bring twiddly pretentious wanker music to the masses.
>
> this is the dream. lets make it happen.

Funnily enough, that's almost exactly what happened. Clever Girl is more popular than ever, and the band reunited for a show when the EP came out on vinyl. They plan to record and release more music and play a few shows. The dream came true. Life, uh, found a way.

•

Many modern-day math rock bands have engaged with the internet from the very beginning, using the web to find new fans, interact with existing ones, and as a tool in their songwriting. Covet's Yvette Young, when her group was just getting started, would use Instagram to incentivize her writing. She'd do this by coming up with a riff and posting it to social media. People would post comments, asking when the whole song would be available. But there was no song, it was just a riff. The positive reaction would push Young to write a song around the riff. Some groups take this even farther, using the web to not only write songs but show others how those songs can be played. TTNG, Giraffes? Giraffes!, and Standards all sell tabs (a sort of sheet music) directly to fans. Some artists post playthroughs or online tutorials that give amateur musicians step-by-step instructions on how to recreate a riff or track. Whereas rock stars like Eddie Van Halen used to be fiercely protective of their techniques and tricks, math rock musicians freely invite anyone, anywhere, to play just like them.

All this online activity can create a ferocious demand. Bands must have a presence on multiple platforms simultaneously, posting often to Facebook, Instagram, YouTube, TikTok, and elsewhere. In addition to the daily grind of creating and uploading new content, the quest then becomes getting noticed. "In some ways it's been amazing for musicians in the sense that they can just get their stuff out there," says author Simon Reynolds. "They can put it on Bandcamp or Soundcloud or even YouTube. But then the challenge is getting attention or getting discovered."

It can be tough when the hoped-for viral video doesn't go viral. Talking to *Sad Planetarium* in 2018 about the difficulties of being a musician, Marcos Mena from Standards talked about the internet. "Small things like not getting as many likes on a video will sometimes make me feel like I don't play as well, or that people prefer another musician to me."

For fans, all this online activity is nothing but a benefit. Communities on Reddit and elsewhere celebrate the genre, and new groups appear almost daily on Bandcamp. On YouTube there are reaction videos, cover versions, explainer videos, and playlists with evocative titles like "japanese math rock to listen while strolling around in the cherry blossoms." Stephen Hazel's YouTube channel Let's Talk About Math Rock has proven so successful since its 2016 launch that the revenue he receives is almost enough to live on. These various online outlets and assets are essential for spreading the gospel of the genre and for helping to create and encourage the next generation of math rock musicians. "I grew up printing NOFX tabs that I printed off a super basic website created by a Finnish guy called Jussi Heinonen," says Foster Parents guitarist Gregor Fair. "I genuinely don't think I would be playing guitar now if it wasn't for that resource. So I get the importance of having these resources when you're starting out and learning."

Twenty years ago, Myspace users discovered new bands by clicking from a friend's page to a band's page. Today, streaming platforms like Spotify save you the trouble by connecting the dots for you. They've also changed the way people think about and consume music. In the past, to listen to a record you had to physically have in your possession a vinyl LP, cassette, or CD. Listeners today don't own anything. Instead, they tap into mind-bogglingly large catalogs of music (for a monthly fee). Ownership is out; access is in.

The online consumption of music has also eased if not began to entirely erase genre boundaries. For performers who had either felt restricted by the box they'd been put into, or who just wanted to straddle several genres at once, this was a liberating concept. "People were finding music in a different way," Santigold told *Stereogum* in 2022. "It didn't have to be 'I went to the record store and I looked into this section, and I identify myself as liking rock. So I'm only going to look in the rock section.' All of a sudden, on the computer, it was all there." Record stores had long been carved into sections like a grapefruit—with different styles relegated to their own individual areas—but streaming sites like Spotify, Pandora, and Apple Music are doing away with all that. At a Spotify event in 2015, founder and CEO Daniel Ek went so far as to declare, "Music is moving away from genres." What it was increasingly moving toward was feelings and moments.

When Spotify first launched in 2006, people had to choose what they wanted to hear. Songza, a streaming service that appeared a year after Spotify, instead asked users to select from six different moods and activities to describe what they were doing at that moment. Depending on a user's choices, Songza would serve up a playlist they thought would match the action. To be as dynamic as possible, Songza's prompts varied by day and time. On Wednesday evening, the user could pick from options like "Driving" and "Spending Time with Your Kids." Late on a Friday this changed to "Making Out" and "Getting High." It was no longer enough to just have a huge database of songs. Streaming services now wanted to create personalized ways of serving up those millions of tracks so that the right one would hit a listener at the right time.

While Songza showed some early success, the site relied on human curators to create playlists. (The company was sold to Google in 2014 and folded into Google Play Music two years later.) With users growing exponentially, streaming services had to come up with algorithms that would provide recommendations at scale. To do this effectively, companies needed to know a lot about you. "Beyond mere personalization," write the authors of *Spotify Teardown*, "the algorithms would also take into account spatial data (where you are), temporal data (the day of the week, the season of the year), and maybe even the weather." Santa Claus may know if you've been bad or good, but Spotify knows what day it is and whether it's snowing or hazy.

The beauty of math rock is that it doesn't lend itself to any of these methods or uses. Whereas most music acts as a kind of veil or shade, the overlay to a moment, math rock *is* the moment. You can't do anything while listening to math rock except listen to it. As a test, sit with a friend while *Don Caballero 2* plays in the background. Think you can have a conversation? You'll be lucky to have a thought. "Safety plays a role for a lot of us in choosing music," writes Daniel J. Levitin in his 2006 book *This Is Your Brain on Music*. "To a certain extent, we surrender to music when we listen to it—we allow ourselves to trust the composers and musicians with a part of our hearts and our spirits; we let the music take us somewhere outside of ourselves." Most listeners only want to be taken to a quiet park on a sunny day. What's being sought is comfort and the assurance that nothing out of place will attack their sensibilities. Math rock doesn't grant that kind of asylum. Bands like Hella and Tera Melos offer the sonic equivalent of a carnival ride or haunted house, not green grass and picnics.

Even though access to millions of songs, along with playlists that seek to cater to our every emotion and frame of mind, sounds like a good thing, a rising number of people are rebelling against the idea of music being reduced to mere metadata. In a *Guardian* article from 2022 about music fans quitting Spotify, several listeners stated that they *experienced* lots of music, but didn't *listen* to any of it. "Before there was streaming music, what else was streaming?" asks New York musician Jared Samuel Elioseff. "This idea that you can just turn on a faucet, and out comes music. It's something that leaves everyone to take it for granted." Not owning anything ironically makes it more disposable, like playing with Monopoly money. "Seeking out music used to be an activity, and it was fun," American Football's Mike Kinsella told *GQ* in 2016. "You did the legwork and you discovered this thing." Putting time into discovering a new band or performer made you appreciate them more. If that legwork now happens digitally, with fans unearthing groups like Clever Girl or Piglet, then the thrill and connection Kinsella talked about remains. When those bands are shared with friends, or even strangers on social media, that joy and fun is multiplied. But when those connections are made automatically, by a computer or algorithm devoid of context, commentary, or community, something is lost.

Despite the genre refusing to be aural wallpaper, or the musical equivalent of stock footage, finding and listening to math rock online makes thematic sense in a way that other genres don't. An afternoon spent on the web means constantly switching between and being bombarded by all kinds of different material. One minute you're mad, the next you're sad. It all adds up to a patchwork, see-saw experience with only the vaguest through line and perhaps no meaning other than it all happened to you within a certain window of time. Math rock—with its constantly shifting time signatures, wildly varying rhythms, and off kilter melodies—is the musical equivalent of that experience.

While streaming services may attempt to flatten and merge all tastes and interests into an algorithmic goo that erases all boundaries, the idea of different kinds of music isn't going away any time soon. "We're never going to get rid of genres," says music historian Theo Cateforis. "The impulse to classify and categorize is human nature." Jeanette Leech, author of

Fearless: The Making of Post-Rock, agrees. "People will always love categorizing, seeking out similar sounding artists, and arguing about who's included and who's not. And if there's one thing the internet does well, it's facilitating arguments." With bands uploading to Bandcamp and YouTube every day complex songs in odd time signatures, math rock's not going away either. The form will only continue to grow and spread, finding new fans and turning on adventurous listeners to pioneers like Don Caballero or new practitioners like Covet. The music that was born and grew in Chicago all those years ago will continue to flourish and spread to every corner of the world. Bands will make the music, and people will call it math rock. Here comes everybody. Let's hope they bring calculators.

8 Cognitive Emancipation: Listening to Math Rock

Math rock has a reputation for being a difficult listen. Given its name, this is inevitable. After all, the reason so many kids in grade school (and beyond) never cared much for the subject is because math is *hard*. Describing the genre to someone usually only makes it worse. The ingredients of long and complicated songs with no vocals, alternate tunings, odd time signatures, and numerous tempo shifts will be seen by most listeners as a negative. "You're asking people to do a lot of work on their first listen," says Rooftops guitarist Drew Fitchette. "It's hard music to get people excited about." Unlike pop music, math rock demands a lot of its audience. But for those who put in the work, the rewards are apparent. "Records you don't like or understand right away, and the ones that take time to decode," adds Fitchette, "typically end up being the ones you fall the hardest in love with."

In a 2017 article in Bangladeshi newspaper *The Daily Star* entitled "Why you should listen to Math Rock," Asif Ayon writes about his conversion to the genre after hearing the track "Path," an early effort by Toe. "It was not like exploring through Rock n' Roll or Jazz because what I had just heard was a mastery of both genres and then some more. I wanted to unravel everything I could about this seemingly alien genre of music especially at a time when I thought guitar music was dead. When I started, I could not stop." For a long time, the only people seemingly willing to take that plunge were fellow musicians. The reason for this was simple: Playing math rock takes serious chops, and only other musicians would know or appreciate the virtuosity on display. "I'm not sure how much we appeal to anyone who doesn't play an instrument," says Pretend drummer Joel Morgan.

Don Caballero drummer Damon Che told me a story about the band's early years that bears this out: "I've had sound personnel come up to the stage to tell us to turn down because it was too loud, and then I would ask, 'Well, why? Do you ask every band to do this? Are we really that loud?' And he'd say, 'You don't understand, all these people in the crowd? They're all *musicians*. Everyone else has left!'"

Over the years, and as the popularity of math rock has grown, with more and more people having been exposed to it through the gentle gateway of twinkly emo bands like American Football, audiences have become more open and willing to take up the challenge. Fourth- and fifth-wave math rock groups now see audiences more willing to embrace them. "We've found that when exposed to it," says Joel Beavin, guitarist for Maryland math rock trio Science Penguin, "a wide variety of people enjoy it even if they didn't think they would."

The first big hurdle people come to when hearing math rock is that most of its songs don't have lyrics. In a live context, this means there's no beautiful rock star up front preening and twirling a microphone. That gap, for many rock fans, feels like a void. "Generally, people want a lead singer to relate to," says author and musician Jon Fine. "People want to sing along." This is easy to understand. Lyrics do several things well. They give a song a subject and a point of view, telling the listener almost instantly what it's about. There's little doubt the classic Hank Williams country tune "I'm So Lonesome I Could Cry" is about someone being so lonesome they could cry (hell, it's all there even in the title). For adventurous listeners, removing all traces of a song's ambiguity is boring; it drains the experience of listening to that song of any sort of mystery, and turns the act into a totally passive experience.

In the English television series *The Mighty Boosh*, which ran on the BBC from 2004 to 2007, Julian Barratt plays a forty-something jazz aficionado named Howard Moon. He lives and works alongside thirty-something Vince Noir. Noir, who loves pop music and worships electro groups like The Human League, declares in an early episode that "only science teachers and the mentally ill" listen to jazz. "You hate jazz?" challenges Moon. "You *fear* jazz. You fear the lack of rules, the lack of boundaries. It has to be simple nursery rhymes for you. When the melody gets abstract, you mess your trousers."

In Moon's view, pop songs are like tract houses: they all look the same, have a roughly similar structure, and are made from parts that are mass-produced and easily identifiable. This makes them boring. Walk into any suburban home and you're likely to encounter a couch and a TV, a few chairs and ottoman. You instantly know you're in the living room. Walk a little further and there's a sink, oven, microwave, counter full of dishes. This is the kitchen. Pop songs are mapped just as easily. Without much effort you can tell which bits are the verses and which is the chorus. Since math rock—like most jazz—is usually devoid of lyrics, and songs don't follow any sort of preset or determined structure, you never know where you are inside of them. This makes for an initially confusing but ultimately liberating experience (if you're willing to be pushed out of your comfort zone). It's like walking into a house and seeing a floor made half out of concrete and half out of wood, with a ladder leading to a hole in the ground and a bag of Fritos containing a parrot hanging by a chain in the ceiling. Would you try to figure out what the hell is going on in a house like that, or would you run for the exit? Many people are like Vince Noir. They want to know where they are in a song, they want to know what it's about. These answers are almost always provided through the vocals. Remove the singer and the words, and listeners often feel lost.

For thousands of years, singing had been a crucial and critical part of music. After its humble beginnings with early humans making noise in caves with instruments made out of bones and hides, most Western music was sung and had an overt religious purpose. Taking inspiration from Jewish synagogues, where Cantors would lead parishioners in the singing of Psalms, early Christian churches continued the tradition by extending the practice to varieties of chanting (Gallican, Gregorian, and so on). These were pieces intended to be sung by a choir or a congregation in a communal setting, no instruments required. In fact, churches shunned musical instruments (except for the organ, and that only made an appearance much later), associating them with pagan rites.

For hundreds of years, ordinary people had neither the means to obtain nor the ability to play the existing instruments of the day. And since the idea of a secular reality was unheard of, any music commissioned or created was both vocal in nature and in benefit to the Church. As the Renaissance segued into the Age of Enlightenment (a period stretching from the fourteenth to the eighteenth centuries), the Church's grip on both the everyday lives of citizens, and art, finally began to loosen. Wealthy aristocrats took the place of the Church in terms of providing patronage to composers and musicians. With the end of the Baroque period, and the beginning of the Classical, which took place around 1750, more and more composers leaned away from vocal music to embrace purely instrumental forms, such as the sonata, symphony, and concerto. Instrumental secular music was suddenly everywhere. An increase in public music festivals and performances also inspired a newly created middle class to take up instruments and make music in their own homes.

A few centuries later, Classical and Romantic composers like Beethoven and Tchaikovsky rolled over to make way for the rock and roll revolution of Chuck Berry, Elvis, and The Beatles. In both Britain and America there was an explosion of instrumental tunes on the pop charts. In 1963 alone, ten instrumental tracks managed to crack the US top ten. Alongside quasi-novelty tunes like "Tequila" by The Champs, whole new genres of instrumental music were created and gained prominence, such as surf music. Groups like The Ventures racked up numerous hits in the sixties. R&B/funk groups, like Booker T. and the M.G.'s, also had high chart positions throughout the decade. But this phenomenon was short-lived. In the seventies and eighties, other than the occasional film soundtrack or TV theme tune, or the odd outlier like Chuck Mangione's 1977 single "Feels So Good," instrumental music mainly disappeared from the pop charts. The last instrumental to hit number one was "Harlem Shake" by Baauer, a track whose popularity was fueled almost exclusively by its use in online memes. While no math rock song has come close to being a hit (cracking the top forty let alone reaching number one), its instrumental nature has paid dividends in other ways.

Music—like dancing or visual art—is its own kind of language, one which can transcend borders. No lyrics means no spoken language; no spoken language means no geographical boundaries. A math rock band from Ecuador can easily be understood and enjoyed by a math rock fan in Hungary, or vice versa. This is why American-made blockbuster movies filled with explosions and car crashes are so popular in non-English-speaking countries; more action means less dialogue. From the beginning, its instrumental nature was the secret ingredient that helped math rock travel the globe.

However, I hasten to make the claim that the genre is truly and completely universal—a form that carries no cultural connotations. Truly universal things are rare if not impossible. Anything invented by humans in one part of the world will retain a seed of that origin as it travels beyond its original region. Math rock, having its roots in both the guitar and genres like jazz and prog, contains in its musical DNA elements of Western thought and traditions; the genre is not quite the blank slate it appears to be.

●

So then, without lyrics to introduce a narrative, protagonist, or subject matter, what are math rock songs about? Without the signposts that vocals provide, how are we to know a song's meaning? This introduces a more fundamental question: do songs *have* to be about anything? Can't they just be sound, appreciated purely for their overall aesthetic appeal or effect? Can't we just enjoy music for its own sake, on its own terms, without assigning to it any sort of explanation or wider significance? The incredible popularity of pop music, versus the relatively limited fanbase of math rock, would seem to answer all these questions rather handily: no.

This gives detractors an easy argument to use against the form, declaring math rock to be the musical equivalent of *Seinfeld*: music about nothing. "It's just guitar noodling! It's just musicians showing off! It doesn't add up to anything!" This isn't true at all.

Listening to math rock is like experiencing any other abstract form of art; its quality is sublime, instinctual, almost primal. Going back to the Jackson Pollock painting on the cover of Ornette Coleman's album *Free Jazz*, that canvas is indeed saying something (as much as any painting can "say something"), it's just not doing so with forms or objects you can instantly identify. Pollock's whole body of work quite effectively conveys a variety of emotions, ranging from anxiety to happiness to rage. Just because the canvases are neither representational nor narrative doesn't mean they're "about nothing" or that they hold no value. "I often felt like there were stories implied in a lot of the songs I've made," says Don Caballero's Ian Williams. "Maybe not so much like, 'And then the boy falls in love with the girl and then they go to the beach.' It's more this vague, abstract story, but it's there. There's still something happening." Drew Fitchette agrees, emphasizing that, in the absence of words or any particular vocal hook to get stuck inside your head, what listeners are drawn to are the melodies. "Don Caballero's a really good example of this. That record *American Don,* to some people, sounds like a wall of noise that makes no sense. But there are grooves that cut through, and melodies that are catchy that really stick in your brain if you listen to it a few times."

Being instrumental, and not being tied to any stated subject, also gives math rock a kind of timelessness. In a song where a character laments a lost love, the listener is made (Howard Moon might say *manipulated*) to feel sad due to the naked emotion that comes from the words and the heart-wrenching performance of the singer. Whether that's Freddie Mercury in 1975 begging a lover not to leave in "Love of My

Life," or Olivia Rodrigo in 2021 declaring to an ex, "You said forever, now I drive alone past your street." By telling us how hurt they are, these singers may get us to connect to a time in our own lives (either past or present) when we felt the same. Sure, it can cut deep, but it's also obvious and one dimensional. Songs rooted in a specific event, either a moment in a listener's life (such as a breakup) or a period in history (think of Dylan's early folk songs about current events) can be like pictures, static and unchanging. There's a potential for the song to lose its meaning over time. Math rock—by not being tied to literal interpretation or an overt emotional state—will never go out of style.

The idea of searching for an explanation to math rock also obscures a perhaps more important topic: how the music makes you *feel*. Kosovo Kusumoto, one of two guitarists for the Japanese band Lite, told *Vice* in 2013, "Rather than having something to say, I want to make the listener feel moved. Rather than moving them with beautiful lyrics or an interesting story, we do it with a tight performance and our sound." Covet's Yvette Young agrees. She told Lee Anderton in a 2019 YouTube interview, "One of the reasons I got into songwriting was because I really enjoy telling stories with sound. "What emotion or mood is stirred in the listener will vary depending on the person receiving the information. This is a type of freedom you don't get in a tune that seeks to tell a literal story. "If you listen to a song like Bobbie Gentry's 'Ode To Billie Joe,'" says Jeanette Leech, author of *Fearless: The Making of Post-Rock*,

> that's a narrative—you start somewhere, you end somewhere else, and Gentry is directing you through her words and the way she has structured the song. You listen to a track like "Scum" by Bark Psychosis, and its aim is not to take you somewhere directed by the

band. It evokes a feeling. I hear a lot of emotion in that track, but it's pretty much up to you what that emotion is and what it sets off in you.

Instead of taking a backseat to the words, math rock musicians are thrust to the foreground, showing their personalities, and speaking through their playing. And yet, whereas a new crop of guitar heroes like Tim Henson from prog metal act Polyphia follows in the footsteps of guys like Steve Vai or Joe Satriani, where songs are ways for them to flex their chops for three to five minutes, math rock bands use musicianship to draw in listeners instead of just trying to wow them with their prowess. "The goosebump feelings when writing a song are sparse," says Pretend's Joel Morgan, "but if we can capture the moment we feel them, maybe the listener can feel them too, in the same way."

A final important by-product that comes from math rock being mostly instrumental is that it forces the music to be interesting. The reason for this simple: If you're going to have a six-minute (or even a two-minute) song that doesn't contain singing or lyrics, it must have other elements that will cause it to hold a listener's interest over the span of its length. This is one of the reasons why math rock songs contain so many different parts and go to a variety of sonic destinations. "Math rock keeps you interested," says Gregor Fair from Foster Parents. "It's like audible Ritalin. I can zone out pretty quickly if the music is too repetitive, which is one thing you can rarely accuse math rock of being."

In an interview from the 2021 free jazz documentary *Fire Music*, musician Cecil Taylor talks about the symbiotic relationship that exists between the genre's players and its fans. "The same way that musicians have to prepare," Taylor says, "listeners have to prepare." Math rock is very much the same. "Math rock expects more of a listener," says music historian Theo Cateforis. Listeners must be engaged and pay attention because math rock, like free jazz and even prog, is all about mystery and suspense. What chord is going to come next? How many more times will the tempo change before the song is finished? Without lyrics or a narrative arc to act as a guide, math rock songs are open worlds where listeners can get lost. Not everyone is up to the challenge. "Math rock appeals to a certain kind of mind," says author Simon Reynolds. "A mind that likes complexity and likes being tested and likes being challenged."

While there's indeed a lot of technicality and complexity in math rock, you don't need to be able to decode or untangle any of it to enjoy the music. Thirty years into its history, this is where modern listeners often get bogged down. Math rock's reputation for being difficult precedes it, and that's enough to keep the curious away. But that needs to all be forgotten.

In Ted Gioia's book *How to Listen to Jazz*, he makes the case for disconnecting music and artists from the burden of both their supposed academic context and their musty historical legacies. The aim is to get would-be fans of the genre to simply open their minds and *hear*. "This is how to listen to Louis Armstrong: Put out of your mind any notion that you are *exploring the tradition* or *revisiting the roots* or *paying tribute to your great grandpa's generation*, or any such hare-brained idea. This is bold, unapologetic music, and by treating it as an antiquated museum piece you are doing it a disservice."

The same goes for math rock. Forget that it's named after your least favorite subject in school, or that many of its players have advanced degrees. Pay no attention to the fact that, even though you may have been playing guitar for decades, you have no idea how these men and women are getting *those* sounds out of *that* instrument. Try not to focus on the structure, or rather the lack of structure, and don't even attempt to count out how many measures are in each bar. Yes, those may be math rock's ingredients, but they're not what's important. You can put it under a microscope if you like and map it out if you have the ability or desire to do so, but that's just extra credit. The only thing that matters is the way math rock makes you *feel*.

Epilogue: Friday Night in Sacramento

It's 2022 and Covet is playing at a small club in midtown called Harlow's that sits at the end of a row of bars, restaurants, and nightclubs. The surrounding streets are rich with history. The state capitol is a just a few blocks away, its bone-white Corinthian columns lit up on this clear night. Right around the corner is Sutter's Fort. Built by slaves, the fort was the first permanent European settlement in the area, and the main economic hub until gold was discovered in 1848. Tonight, homeless people gather in the shadows of its whitewashed walls, curling up in grimy sleeping bags to combat the cold. It's only early November, but there's a chill in the air. Bouncers exhale clouds of steam as they check IDs, while the sound of rap and salsa—along with gusts of heat—seeps from glass doors as they're opened and closed by revelers up and down J Street.

Inside Harlow's, a capacity crowd has gathered for the first night of Covet's fall tour. Earlier in the week the midterm elections were held. So far, the Democrats have had a strong showing; it looks like they're going to keep control of the Senate, maybe even the House. Plus Thanksgiving's in just a few weeks, and Christmas is right around the corner from that. People are feeling good, the mood in the air optimistic. Too optimistic; even though COVID's still killing dozens of people a day, most people aren't wearing masks.

People are packed shoulder to shoulder in front of the small stage, the club's low ceiling making the room feel even more crowded than it really is. Busy bartenders run around wearing shirts that mimic the famous Ramones logo; in place of the band's name, it says HARLOWS. Even though most people are sipping beers, the bar serves rock-themed drinks such as a Raspberry Beret and a non-alcoholic cocktail called Like a Virgin.

It's a diverse crowd. One young kid upfront in a gray sweatshirt also wears a backwards baseball cap that says *America's NAVY forged by the sea*. Another sports a T-shirt from Polyphia's recent world tour. An older guy just a few feet from the college kids looks to be sixty. He's wearing a coffee-colored leather jacket and steel-rimmed glasses, his long greying hair pulled back in a ponytail.

Before the show, new bassist Brandon Dove and drummer Jessica Burdeaux emerge from backstage to check their instruments. Burdeaux's wearing plaid pants and a black t-shirt. Dove has on a brown cap as well as jeans and a white t-shirt under a dark button up, sleeves pushed up past his elbows. While Dove tunes his five-string bass, Burdeaux hits various drums on her four-piece Ludwig. When Yvette Young briefly appears to look over her two guitars, the crowd hoots and hollers for their hero.

Tonight almost didn't happen. After a UK summer tour, Covet's original bassist and drummer both left the band. Fans wondered whether Covet would continue as a group, or turn into a kind of Yvette Young solo act. Young herself wasn't even sure. In the weeks before the tour, she considered scrapping the project altogether. Instead, she drafted in new members, booked a run of shows she's christened the "Rebirth" tour, and decided to give the band one more shot. Hanging behind the stage is a huge hand-painted banner awash in sunset colors. It features a flock of birds flying over the word REBIRTH. The next four weeks will see Covet hit a bunch of secondary markets and venues, places they've mostly never played before. This means shunning big cities like Los Angeles, San Francisco, and New York for smaller towns such as Tucson, Omaha, and Birmingham.

As if having a whole new lineup wasn't difficult enough, last Saturday a 2007 Ford E350 van Young had purchased with her own money specifically for the tour was stolen out of a recording studio parking lot in Oakland. While the band had been inside laying down tracks, someone hotwired the van and drove it away. Young was suddenly out fifteen grand, and had to scramble to rent new transportation in time for tonight's gig. Thankfully, she both found a replacement and raised enough money to pay for it using a GoFundMe page.

After Young returns to the backstage area, Dove and Burdeaux confer with a pair of bearded stagehands over a MacBook placed to the right of the drummer. The issue finally sorted out, bassist and drummer join Young backstage. When the group reappears ten minutes later, the sold-out crowd erupts with applause and cheers. Young grabs one of her two signature Ibanez electric guitars. The color is officially "orange cream sparkle" but, in the darkness of the club, the instrument looks more red than orange. It matches her tomato soup red cardigan and plaid miniskirt. Using a lime green cord, she plugs the Ibanez into a big Vox amp sitting at an angle. At her feet is a pedal board that boasts sixteen stomp boxes.

For the first song, Dove plays an electric violin instead of his bass. The tune starts out soft and spacey, almost ambient. While Young taps out twinkly notes, a capo at the second fret, Burdeaux plays lightly on the drums. For the second song,

Epilogue

Dove picks up his bass and Young starts shredding as Burdeaux pounds on the drums. The band's sound, so clean and bright on record, tonight is raw and loud, more *rock* than *math*. The third song has vocals, but Young's singing can't be heard above the noise of the instruments. Throughout the night there are also backing tracks coming from the laptop—organ and bits of synth—but these accents are drowned out by the volume of the two guitars and drums.

It's kind of amazing this is the first time the three musicians have performed together on stage. The complicated songs flow and ebb without any one of the musicians missing a beat. The sound is tight, muscular, confident. All three players are all smiles. Even when Young stops a song after just a few seconds, complaining she's getting some weird sounds via her in-ear monitors, she just smiles and starts again.

Halfway through the set, Young trades out her orange guitar for a green one. Under the club's blue lights, the slime green looks positively Day-Glo. The band jumps from song to song, Young not stopping to introduce them or even say their names. The crowd doesn't care; they're engrossed in each note.

As Young's fingers fly up and down the fretboard with lightning speed, it's easy to see why she's the poster child for contemporary math rock. Her playing is super technical, highly musical, and jaw-droppingly fast. And yet Young's mastery of the instrument never seems boring or academic, and the songs aren't just vehicles for her to endlessly solo. There are riffs, to be sure, and plenty of runs and melodic phrases, but—like the best math rock—what the band's playing feels like *songs* and not just showing off.

As she performs, Young flashes one of her many tattoos, script that runs alongside the bottom of her right forearm: *to exist in the world but not live in it*. In addition to more tattoos on her arms and legs, she also has tattoos on each finger of her left hand, big X's on the middle digits. She herself had a brief stint as a tattoo artist.

Throughout the night, the band premieres several new songs. The material is ferocious, Young sometimes sounding like Tera Melos's Nick Reinhart. The audience doesn't care that they've never heard these songs before; everything sounds great, and the band is on fire. Announcing the last of the new tunes, Young tells the crowd that it's okay to dance. However, the ensuing song has so many starts, stops, and tempo shifts that dancing is difficult. People just shout instead.

Two decades ago, when Don Caballero played the Fireside Bowl on that Friday night in Chicago, cell phones existed, but they were primitive, expensive, and generally beyond the reach of the crowd of Gen Xers watching the band that night. This meant the audience couldn't do much besides watch the band or talk to their friends. Other than the gear on stage, the only other bit of technology in the room was a guy standing in the back with a bulky camcorder, videotaping the show. Back then, trying to record even a snippet of a concert was a forbidden act. Bands frowned on it, and bouncers would pull you out of a crowd if they saw a video camera or tape recorder. Tonight, pretty much everyone in the crowd at some point holds up their phones to capture a portion of the show. A guy standing next to me sipped Liquid Death all night and recorded most of the hour-long performance. What had once been a communal event restricted to just those in the room can now be instantly uploaded to YouTube and Instagram. It's just another way that's helping math rock expand its influence around the world.

Covet doesn't do encores, so instead Young announces they'll just play an extra song. "This is kind of random," she adds, "but do you guys want a French lesson? This song is kind of a French lesson." As various audience members shout out short phrases in what seems to be passable French, a recorded voice gives the definition of *denouement*. Then the band kicks in, playing one more killer tune. It's the perfect choice, indeed acting as a satisfying conclusion to the evening.

After the final song, all three hug and take bows. Young makes the shape of a heart with her hands and points it at the audience. Rebirth. The crowd feels the joy. People continue to clap and cheer as the members of Covet retreat backstage, leaving behind their instruments and the painting of birds. Young's been fascinated with birds for years; to this day, they're a big part of her art. The first Covet LP, painted by Young, featured a dozen birds, and merch for tonight's show is replete with avian imagery on T-shirts and hoodies. As a child, she raised birds as pets and spent hours drawing them; even now, as an adult, she keeps them as pets. Young admired their natural beauty, the symmetry of their wings, the color of their feathers. But she was also envious of their freedom. As a child who often felt trapped by the high expectations of her parents, she was jealous of birds. If they wanted to, they could just fly away. Escape. Go, literally, anywhere.

That independence has been considered the holy grail by musicians for decades. It's what caused Ornette Coleman to throw out almost everything contained in the jazz rulebook and start a whole new style that contained the word "free" right in the name. It's what encouraged prog bands to turn their back on the three-minute pop song, crafting instead twenty-minute epics that took up an entire side of vinyl. It's what pushed hardcore bands to transform the raw energy of punk and metal into the pounding, intricate precision of thrash. That freedom is a huge part of math rock. That smile on Young's face tonight is because she's finally become the bird she spent years dreaming about. Free from the standard pop format, free from any formal constraints, free to travel anywhere musically her imagination can take her. And if the price of that freedom means not having a hit song, playing clubs instead of arenas, or trading millions of fans for thousands of them, who cares? It's worth it.

10 Essential Tracks

1. Don Caballero, "In The Absence Of Strong Evidence To The Contrary, One May Step Out Of The Way Of The Charging Bull" 1998

While you can debate whether math rock definitively began with Don Caballero, what can't be argued is that the Chicago-by-way-of-Pittsburgh group were one of the best (and earliest) practitioners of the form. Taken from the band's third LP, *What Burns Never Returns*, this song has everything math rock has come to be known for: a long and inscrutable title, odd time signatures, tempo shifts, and tons of fingertapping.

2. Piglet, "Little Bubble, Where You Going?" 2005

After Don Caballero set the template for what later came to be known as math rock, for the next few years the sound was confined to a handful of Chicago bands, most of which didn't last long. Piglet was one of them. The trio recorded just a half-dozen songs, and played only a handful of shows, but they've gone on to be incredibly influential.

3. Toe, "孤独の発明 (Invention of Loneliness)" 2005

After a succession of midwestern groups released just one record and then broke up (Piglet, Dakota/Dakota, Lynx, Ghosts, and Vodka), Toe became the first math rock band to stick around. The fact that they're from Japan shows how the math rock sound, previously restricted to America, traveled internationally. (Extra credit: listen for the scream at 2:40.)

4. Tera Melos, "40 Rods to the Hog's Head" 2007

With guitar, drums, and bass that go batshit crazy for pretty much the entirety of the track's more than eight-minute running time, this is the closest the genre comes to free jazz. Not only does this sound like four or five different songs, but it also sounds like more than one track playing *at the same time*. But it's not just noise; "40 Rods" ebbs and flows, rises and falls, creating a journey that acts as a sort of mini history of the entire genre.

5. Rooftops, "Year As Lift" 2009

This song, from the Washington band's lone album, *A Forest of Polarity*, shows how math rock groups—who most often don't feature singers or songs with lyrics—make use of words and language. Every song title on the LP is an anagram for "Fairy Tales" ("Tear As I Fly," "A Layer Fits," "Leafy Star," and so on), while the record's title is itself an anagram for "Rooftops Fairy Tales." As if all that linguistic trickery isn't enough, the first initial of all ten songs spell out FAIRY TALES.

6. Clever Girl, "Elm" 2010

This five piece from Sheffield, England is yet another math rock group who played a few shows, recorded an EP, and promptly broke up. The group, which features two guitars, drums, bass, and saxophone, strays from the hard rock edges of Don Caballero and Tera Melos, leaning much more into jazz.

7. Elephant Gym, "Finger" 2013

Every member of this Taiwanese trio was classically trained. The core of the group consists of siblings KT and Tell Chang, KT on bass, and Tell on electric guitar. Formed in 2012, Elephant Gym have toured the world and recorded numerous albums (with *Dreams*, from 2022, being the most recent). "Finger," the first song from 2013 EP *Balance*, starts with KT performing fluid taps on her bass guitar (the song's title is most likely a reference to the fact that most of math rock's riffs, and complicated runs, are plucked with fingers rather than picks).

8. Foster Parents, "Colors Casted" 2017

Foster Parents, a duo of English ex-pats living in China, have produced an LP and three EPs. Their stellar 2017 album *Grim*, which came out on a tiny Chinese label, is impossible to find in any physical format but is on streaming services and YouTube. Foster Parents lace their tracks with snatches of dialogue from eighties teen films like *Weird Science* and *The Karate Kid*. This adds to the tunes a layer of nostalgia, while also providing the emotional heft or humor that lyrics often provide.

9. Cuzco, "Larrie's Sandwich" 2019

Despite only releasing one album and a pair of EPs, North Carolina's Cuzco made a big contribution to the catalog of math rock. Their highly melodic and intricate songs, which pair crystalline guitar lines with soft horns, are very much in the vibe and style of Clever Girl (the band acknowledged their debt to the English group in the 2017 track "We Miss You Clever Girl," itself a reference to a song by Weye dedicated to another group that didn't last long called "We Miss You Piglet").

10. Covet, "Firebird" 2023

Covet's guitarist and main songwriter Yvette Young is a brilliantly adept player who mixes classical training with a fluid fingertapping style that's a direct descendent from Ian William's fretwork in Don Caballero. And while Young has long been obsessed with avian imagery, incorporating birds into the band's record covers and merchandise, this track's title has a more direct and simple meaning. Says Young, "I named this song after the first car my mom bought when she arrived in the US." Her parents were Chinese immigrants who worked multiple jobs to pay for violin and piano lessons, in addition to purchasing the red Pontiac Firebird which is the inspiration for this song.

References

Chapter 1: All Is Number

"John Stanier from Battles Reads Obscure Comments about Himself," *YouTube*, uploaded by *The Drummer's Journal*, September 24, 2015. https://www.youtube.com/watch?v=nvYb1-Tvcvl

LeMay, Matt. "Chavez," *Pitchfork*, December 6, 2006. https://pitchfork.com/features/interview/6502-chavez

Cavanaugh, Joanne P. "Arithmetic of the Soul," *Johns Hopkins Magazine*, February 1998. https://pages.jh.edu/jhumag/0298web/math.html

Du Sautoy, Marcus. "Listen by Numbers: Music and Maths," *The Guardian*, June 27, 2011. https://www.theguardian.com/music/2011/jun/27/music-mathematics-fibonacci

Lliraels. "Finally, a Music Genre That Sounds Like the Inside of My Brain," *Reddit*, October 4, 2021. https://www.reddit.com/r/mathrock/comments/q1i2sh/finally_a_music_genre_that_sounds_like_the_inside

Chapter 2: Breadcrumb Trail

Woodward, Richard B. "Cormac McCarthy's Venomous Fiction," *New York Times*, April 19, 1992. https://www.nytimes.com/1992/04/19/magazine/cormac-mccarthy-s-venomous-fiction.html

Shteamer, Hank. "King Crimson's '21st Century Schizoid Man':
Inside Prog's Big Bang," *Rolling Stone*, October 1, 2019. https://
www.rollingstone.com/music/music-features/king-crimson-
interview-writing-21st-century-schizoid-man–891600

Sanneh, Kelefa, "The Persistence of Prog Rock," *The New
Yorker*, June 12, 2017. https://www.newyorker.com/
magazine/2017/06/19/the-persistence-of-prog-rock

Palmer, Robert. "Black Flag Adds a Soupcon of Sophistication to
Punk Rock," *New York Times*, February 23, 1986. https://www.
nytimes.com/1986/02/23/arts/black-flag adds-a-soupcon-of-
sophistication-to-punk-rock.html

Chapter 3: Rollerblade Success Story

Smith, Ethan. "Music Review: 'Ride the Fader,'" *Entertainment
Weekly*, November 8, 1996. https://ew.com/
article/1996/11/08/music-review-ride-fader

Despres, Shawn. "Math Rockers Toe Take It Slow," *The Japan
Times*, January 29, 2010. https://www.japantimes.co.jp/
culture/2010/01/29/music/math-rockers-toe-take-it-slow

Robson, Daniel. "Mike Watt Loves Japanese Math Rockers Lite and
So Do We," *Vice*, August 27, 2013a. https://www.vice.com/en/
article/6anger/mike-watt loves-japanese math-rockers-lite-
and-so-do-we

Smith, James. "INTERVIEW: This Town Needs Guns," *God Is in
the TV*, January 22, 2013. https://www.godisinthetvzine.
co.uk/2013/01/22/interview-this-town-needs-guns

Chapter 4: Oh Messy Life

Reynolds, Simon. "American Alternative Rock: A Survey of the State of the Art," *Reynolds Retro*, October 15, 2007. https://reynoldsretro.blogspot.com/2007/10/american-alternative-rock-survey-of.html

Driveshaft1982. "Song Discussion—Like Herod (Mogwai Young Team)," *Reddit*, May 7, 2020. https://www.reddit.com/r/mogwaiband/comments/gf78ky/song_discussion_like_herod_mogwai_young_team

"Here Are the 20 Best Mathcore Albums of All Time," *The Pit*, August 12, 2020. https://www.wearethepit.com/2020/08/here-are-the-20-best-mathcore-albums-of-all-time

Necci, Marilyn Drew. "Behold the Arctopus: The Only Band That Has Homework Assignments," *RVA Mag*, March 15, 2013. https://rvamag.com/music/behold-the-arctopus-the-only-band-that-has-homework-assignments.html

Segerstrom, Christian. "Interview with Colin Marston of Behold the Arctopus," *Mathcore Index*, September 11, 2019. https://mathcoreindex.com/2019/09/11/interview-colin-marston-of-behold-the-arctopus

Freeman, Phil. "Behold the Arctopus," *Burning Ambulance*, June 30, 2020. https://burningambulance.com/2020/06/30/behold-the-arctopus

"What Killed Mathcore?" *YouTube*, uploaded by The Punk Rock MBA, October 4, 2021. https://www.youtube.com/watch?v=KSpwoolz8Is

"Notes from the Underground," *Thrasher Magazine*, January 1986. https://www.thrashermagazine.com/articles/magazine/january–1986

Rogers, Nate. "Who's Afraid of Being Called Emo?" *The Ringer*, July 27, 2022. https://www.theringer.com/music/2022/7/27/23279669/bands-not-wanting-to-be-called-emo-history

Brannon, Norman. "Emo: A Personal History in Three Parts—Part 1, 1987–1990," *Talkhouse*, July 16, 2019. https://www.talkhouse.com/emo-a-personal-history-in-three-parts-part-1-1987–1990

Mullen, Matt. "The Secret History of Emo Music," *Interview*, December 5, 2017. https://www.interviewmagazine.com/music/secret-history-emo-music

Chapter 5: Savage Composition

Ratsimbaharison, Ony. "Eve Alpert of Palm on Exploring Time Signatures and Meter," *She Shreds*, August 16, 2017. https://sheshreds.com/musicians-tips-palm

Koshanin. "Odd Meters and Time Signatures in Music—Part 1," *Koshanin's Blog*, July 27, 2013. https://koshanin.com/blog/2018/07/23/odd-meters-and-time-signatures-in-music-part–1

Lekas, Noah. "Tim Kinsella: The Aquarium Drunkard Interview," *Aquarium Drunkard*, August 30, 2022. https://aquariumdrunkard.com/2022/08/30/tim-kinsella-the-aquarium-drunkard-interview

"The Damon Che Interviews—American Don." *YouTube*, uploaded by Don Caballero Official, August 19, 2021. https://www.youtube.com/watch?v=tt6Dw6npuwk

"We are the band GIRAFFES? GIRAFFES! and we invite you to ASK US ANYTHING! AMA AUA," *Reddit*, July 18, 2018. https://www.

reddit.com/r/mathrock/comments/8zvi4l/we_are_the_band_giraffes_giraffes_and_we_invite

Chan, M. "Floral—Floral LP," *The Math Rock Times*. https://www.mathrocktimes.com/single-post/floral-floral-lp

Safran Foer, Jonathan. "Jonathan Safran Foer on Paul Muldoon," *Poetry Society of America*. https://poetrysociety.org/poems-essays/tributes/jonathan-safran-foer-on-paul-muldoon

Bennett, David. "Mike Kinsella on the Surprising Comeback of American Football," *Miami New Times*, July 30, 2018. https://www.miaminewtimes.com/music/american-football-at-revolution-live–10567223

Henkin, Greg. "Interview: Mike Kinsella," *Greg's Guitar Lessons*, November 8, 2011. https://gregsguitarlessons.com/2011/11/08/mike-kinsella-owen

Lynham, Alex. "Giraffes? Giraffes!'s Joseph Andreoli: 'Our Music Is Technical at Times, It's Dissonant at Times, but There's This Playfulness,'" *Music Radar*, September 11, 2018. https://www.musicradar.com/news/giraffes-giraffess-joseph-andreoli-our-music-is-technical-at-times-its-dissonant-at-times-but-theres-this-playfulness

Chapter 6: Tremolo + Delay

Cortina, Lene. "This Is a Chord," *Punk Girl Diaries*, January 9, 2018. https://punkgirldiaries.com/this-is-a-chord

Bosso, Joe. "Steve Hackett: How I invented Finger Tapping," *Music Radar*, April 30, 2012. https://www.musicradar.com/news/guitars/steve-hackett-how-i-invented-finger-tapping–542029

Kompanek, Christopher. "Guitarist Marnie Stern Takes a Melodic Turn on 'The Chronicles of Marnia,'" *The Washington Post*, May

2, 2013. https://www.washingtonpost.com/goingoutguide/
guitarist-marnie-stern-takes-a-melodic-turn-on-the-
chronicles-of-marnia/2013/05/01/2ca70188-ac2b-11e2-b6fd-
ba6f5f26d70e_story.html

"The Captain Meets Yvette Young." *YouTube*, uploaded by
Andertons Music Co, December 15, 2019. https://www.
youtube.com/watch?v=jSxL7zOzY30&t=902s

Whiteside, Michael. "Telecasters & Math Rock: A Narrative
History," *Fecking Bahamas*, September 26, 2019. https://
feckingbahamas.com/focus-telecasters-math-rock-a-narrative-
history

"Giraffes? Giraffes! x Curse League—Band to Band Interview," *The
Math Rock Times*. https://www.mathrocktimes.com/single-
post/2018/08/09/giraffes-giraffes-x-curse-league-band-to-
band-interview

Chapter 7: Here Comes Everybody

Cohn, David. "Bands Embrace Social Networking," *Wired*, May
18, 2005. https://www.wired.com/2005/05/bands-embrace-
social-networking

Schneider, Jacqueline. "How Myspace Opened the Door to Niche
Music Genres," *Forbes*, March 20, 2019. https://www.forbes.
com/sites/jacquelineschneider/2019/03/20/how-myspace-
opened-the-door-to-niche-music-genres

Hyland, Samuel. "The Band That the Internet Remembered,"
Sammysworld. https://sammysworld.org/the-band-that-the-
internet-remembered

Covert, William. "*Spiderland: A Math Rock Classic Turns 25*," *Fecking
Bahamas*, March 26, 2016. https://feckingbahamas.com/focus-
spiderland-a-math-rock-classic-turns-25

Zhang, Margaret. "Marcos Mena: From Math to Mozart," *Sad Planetarium*, September 19, 2018. https://www. sadplanetarium.com/interviews/2018/9/19/marcos-mena-from-math-to-mozart

Brodsky, Rachel. "We've Got a File on You: Santigold," *Stereogum*, September 1, 2022. https://www.stereogum.com/2197911/santigold-spirituals/interviews/weve-got-a-file-on-you

Pelly, Liz. "'There's Endless Choice, but You're Not Listening': Fans Quitting Spotify to Save Their Love of Music," *The Guardian*, September 27, 2022. https://www.theguardian.com/music/2022/sep/27/theres-endless-choice-but-youre-not-listening-fans-quitting-spotify-to-save-their-love-of-music

Woolf, Jake. "Exclusive: American Football Premieres Its New Song 'Desire Gets in the Way,'" *GQ*, October 4, 2016. https://www.gq.com/story/american-football-new-song-desire-gets-in-the-way-mike-kinsella

Chapter 8: Cognitive Emancipation

Ayon, Asif. "Why You Should Listen to Math Rock," *The Daily Star*, November 2, 2017. https://www.thedailystar.net/shout/music/why-you-should-listen-math-rock–1484899

Robson, Daniel. "Mike Watt Loves Japanese Math Rockers Lite and So Do We," *Vice*, August 27, 2013b. https://www.vice.com/en/article/6anger/mike-watt-loves-japanese-math-rockers-lite-and-so-do-we

"The Captain Meets Yvette Young," *YouTube*, uploaded by Andertons Music Co, December 15, 2019. https://www.youtube.com/watch?v=jSxL7zOzY30&t=902s

Farber, Jim. "'It Didn't Adhere to Any of the Rules': The Fascinating History of Free Jazz," *The Guardian*, September 7, 2021. https://www.theguardian.com/film/2021/sep/07/fire-music-history-free-jazz-documentary

Ten Essential Tracks

Young, Yvette [@youyve]. "I Named this Song after the First Car my mom bought when she arrived in the US." *Twitter*, February 21, 2023, https://twitter.com/youyve/status/1628267031769513984